Crack the Embedded Syste

101 Questions & Answers for Job Seekers

By
Sarful Hassan

Preface

Welcome to *Crack the Embedded Systems Interview: 101 Questions & Answers for Job Seekers*. This book is the result of years of experience in embedded systems development, teaching, and interview preparation. It was written with the goal of helping learners and professionals succeed in technical interviews and build a strong foundation in embedded concepts.

Who This Book Is For

- Engineering students and recent graduates preparing for job interviews
- Job seekers targeting roles in embedded systems, IoT, firmware, and microcontroller programming
- Professionals switching into embedded domains from related technical fields
- Educators and trainers seeking structured content for embedded systems courses

How This Book Is Organized

The book is divided into five logical sections:

1. **Embedded Systems Fundamentals (Q1–25)** – Definitions, architecture, memory, microcontrollers vs microprocessors
2. **Embedded C & Programming Concepts (Q26–50)** – C programming, pointers, memory, recursion, ISRs
3. **Microcontroller Peripherals & Protocols (Q51–75)** – UART, SPI, I2C, ADC/DAC, GPIO, DMA
4. **Debugging & Tools (Q76–90)** – Oscilloscopes, JTAG, IDEs, simulations, logic analyzers
5. **Real-World Scenarios & Projects (Q91–101)** – Low-power design, OTA updates, RTOS, project samples

Each question is followed by a detailed answer that explains not just the 'what,' but also the 'how' and 'why'.

What Was Left Out

This book focuses on **interview preparation**, not in-depth academic theory or extensive device datasheets. We also avoided proprietary tools and vendor-specific content in favor of general, industry-relevant knowledge.

Code Style (About the Code)

All code examples are written in **Embedded C** with clarity and simplicity in mind. They are formatted for readability and follow common conventions used in industry:

- Variables and functions are named descriptively
- Code snippets are tested or pseudocode unless otherwise noted
- Hardware-specific code assumes general microcontroller knowledge (e.g., STM32, AVR, ESP32)

Release Notes

First Edition - April 2025

- 101 interview questions and answers
- Structured by topic and complexity
- Includes practical guidance and real-world examples

Notes on the First Edition

This is the first edition of this book. We welcome your feedback to improve future updates and editions. If you find errors or have suggestions, please contact us.

MechatronicsLAB Online Learning

Explore more learning content, video lectures, and hands-on embedded projects at:

- ☐ Website: mechatronicslab.net
- ✉@ Email: mechatronicslab.net@gmail.com

How to Contact Us

We welcome feedback, corrections, and collaboration ideas:

- Email: **mechatronicslab.net@gmail.com**
- Website: **www.mechatronicslab.net**

Acknowledgments for the First Edition

Special thanks to the contributors, reviewers, and students whose feedback shaped this book. Gratitude to our early readers and the embedded systems community for inspiring its creation.

Copyright (MechatronicsLAB)

Disclaimer

This book is provided for educational and interview preparation purposes. While every effort has been made to ensure accuracy, the author and publisher are not responsible for errors or omissions, or for any loss incurred as a result of the use of this book.

Table of Contents

Section 1: Embedded Systems Fundamentals (1–25)

Interview Question 1: What Is an Embedded System?

Why This Question Is Asked: This is a fundamental technical question often asked in interviews for electronics, software, and hardware-related roles. It tests your understanding of core concepts and whether you can explain them clearly.

What the Interviewer Wants to Know:

- Do you understand what an embedded system is?
- Can you explain it in simple, accurate terms?
- Are you aware of its applications and characteristics?

How to Structure Your Answer:

1. Define what an embedded system is
2. Mention key features or components
3. Give real-world examples or use cases

Sample Answer (Beginner): "An embedded system is a computer system designed to perform a specific task within a larger device. It usually includes a processor, memory, and input/output peripherals, all integrated into one system. Unlike general-purpose computers, embedded systems are built for dedicated functions — like controlling a microwave, ATM, or smart thermostat."

Sample Answer (Experienced): "An embedded system is a combination of hardware and software designed for a dedicated function within a larger mechanical or electrical system. It typically operates with real-time constraints and minimal user interaction. Examples include automotive engine control units, medical devices, and industrial automation controllers. Embedded systems are optimized for performance, size, and efficiency."

Do and Don't Section

Do:

- ✅ Define it clearly and concisely
- ✅ Use real-world examples (microwaves, smartwatches, cars)
- pecific traits like real-time processing or limited resources

Don't:

- ❌ Use overly complex jargon (unless asked for deep technical depth)
- ❌ Confuse embedded systems with general-purpose computers
- ❌ Skip giving an example or practical context

Beginner Tip: If you're new to embedded systems, focus on understanding how simple everyday devices like digital clocks or washing machines rely on them to perform automatic functions.

Final Thought: This question is a chance to show both clarity and technical insight. A confident, simple explanation with solid examples shows you grasp the core concept — and can communicate it effectively.

Interview Question 2: How Does an Embedded System Differ from a General-Purpose System?

Why This Question Is Asked: Interviewers use this question to test your conceptual clarity about embedded systems and to see if you can distinguish them from general computing systems in terms of design, functionality, and application.

What the Interviewer Wants to Know:

- Can you define both systems clearly?
- Do you understand their differences in terms of purpose, resources, and user interaction?
- Can you provide relevant examples?

How to Structure Your Answer:

1. Define both embedded and general-purpose systems
2. Highlight key differences (use a comparison table if helpful)
3. Provide real-life examples for each

Sample Answer: "An embedded system is a specialized computer designed to perform a specific task within a larger system. It typically has limited resources, minimal user interface, and often operates under real-time constraints. Examples include microwave controllers, digital watches, and automotive ECUs.

In contrast, a general-purpose system, like a desktop or laptop computer, is built to perform a wide range of tasks. It has more processing power, memory, and a rich user interface. Examples include Windows PCs, Linux servers, and MacBooks."

Comparison Table:

Feature	Embedded System	General-Purpose System
Purpose	Specific task	Multiple tasks
Resources	Limited (CPU, RAM, storage)	High (powerful CPU, large memory)
User Interface	Minimal or none	Full GUI or CLI
Real-time Operation	Often required	Rarely required
Examples	Washing machine, thermostat	Laptop, desktop

Do and Don't Section

Do:

- ✓ Clearly define and compare both systems
- ✓ Use a table to make differences easy to grasp
- ✓ Mention real-world examples

Don't:

- ✗ Be vague or use buzzwords without explanation
- ✗ Forget to highlight application areas
- ✗ Assume prior knowledge — explain as if to a beginner

Beginner Tip: Think of your mobile phone's camera processor (embedded system) vs. your phone's main operating system (general-purpose). Both are in the same device but serve different purposes.

Final Thought: This question highlights your ability to draw clear distinctions and explain technical differences. A thoughtful answer shows both depth and clarity of understanding.

Interview Question 3: What Are the Key Components of an Embedded System?

Why This Question Is Asked: This question evaluates your understanding of the internal structure and functioning parts of an embedded system. It's fundamental for roles in embedded software and hardware development.

What the Interviewer Wants to Know:

- Do you know what makes up an embedded system?
- Can you explain how these components work together?
- Are you aware of both hardware and software elements?

How to Structure Your Answer:

1. Mention the core hardware components
2. Include key software elements
3. Briefly explain the role of each component

Sample Answer: "An embedded system typically consists of both hardware and software components. The main hardware elements include:

1. **Processor (Microcontroller or Microprocessor):** The brain of the system, responsible for executing instructions.
2. **Memory (RAM and ROM):** RAM is used for temporary data storage; ROM holds the firmware.
3. **Input Devices:** Sensors, buttons, or any mechanism to receive input from the external environment.
4. **Output Devices:** LEDs, displays, actuators, or other mechanisms to send feedback or results.
5. **Communication Interfaces:** Such as UART, SPI, or I2C for data exchange with other devices or systems.

On the software side:

1. **Firmware/Embedded Software:** The program running on the hardware, usually stored in ROM.
2. **Operating System (optional):** Many embedded systems use a Real-Time Operating System (RTOS) to manage tasks.

All these components work together to perform the system's dedicated function efficiently and reliably."

Do and Don't Section

Do:

- ✅ Break down the answer into hardware and software parts
- ✅ Give real-world examples where applicable
- ✅ Explain how the components interrelate

Don't:

- ✖ Just list components without explanation
- ✖ Mix up roles (e.g., saying RAM stores firmware)
- ✖ Skip software components — they are just as important

Beginner Tip: Start by understanding a microcontroller development board like Arduino or STM32 — they include almost all the key components you'll need to recognize.

Final Thought: This is a great opportunity to show a clear, structured understanding of embedded architecture. Listing components is good — explaining their function and integration is even better.

Interview Question 4: Give Examples of Embedded Systems in Daily Life

Why This Question Is Asked: Interviewers ask this to check your practical understanding of embedded systems. It's not just about theory — they want to see if you can connect it to the real world.

What the Interviewer Wants to Know:

- Are you familiar with real-world applications of embedded systems?
- Can you categorize them across industries or usage types?
- Do you understand the role of embedded systems in these examples?

How to Structure Your Answer:

1. Start with a brief introduction
2. List categories (e.g., home, automotive, medical, industrial, consumer electronics)
3. Provide 2–3 examples in each category
4. Optionally explain what the embedded system does in each case

Sample Answer: "Embedded systems are everywhere in our daily lives, often hidden within devices to perform specific functions. Here are some examples across different domains:
Home Appliances:

- Microwave ovens: Embedded controller handles time, power, and heating cycles
- Washing machines: Controls drum speed, water intake, and washing logic
- Smart thermostats: Regulate room temperature based on sensors and user input

Automotive:

- Engine Control Units (ECUs): Manage engine performance and fuel injection
- Anti-lock Braking System (ABS): Ensures safe braking
- Airbag control modules: Detect collision and deploy airbags

Medical Devices:

- Digital thermometers: Measure and display temperature accurately
- Pacemakers: Monitor and regulate heart rhythm
- Blood glucose monitors: Measure sugar levels and display readings

Consumer Electronics:

- Smartphones: Embedded chips control camera, battery, and sensors
- Smart TVs: Embedded OS manages video playback and network connectivity
- Fitness trackers: Monitor steps, heart rate, and sleep patterns

Industrial Automation:

- Programmable Logic Controllers (PLCs): Control machines and processes
- Robotic arms: Perform precise and repetitive tasks
- Sensor modules: Monitor temperature, pressure, and motion

These systems are optimized for the task they're designed to do and operate reliably with minimal user intervention."

Do and Don't Section

Do:

- ✓ Cover multiple industries for diversity
- ✓ Explain what the system does in a few cases
- ✓ Keep it clear and relatable

Don't:

- ✗ Mention too many technical details
- ✗ Forget to mention the task the system performs
- ✗ Limit your examples to only one category

Beginner Tip: Try observing everyday devices around you — anything that works automatically with minimal user input likely has an embedded system inside.

Final Thought: This is a chance to show you can connect theory to reality. Diverse, well-explained examples demonstrate not only knowledge but insight into how embedded systems impact modern life.

Interview Question 5: What Are the Classifications of Embedded Systems?

Why This Question Is Asked: This question helps interviewers assess your deeper understanding of the diversity and scope of embedded systems. It shows whether you know how they are categorized based on function, performance, and complexity.

What the Interviewer Wants to Know:

- Can you identify the main types of embedded systems?
- Do you understand the basis of classification?
- Can you provide examples for each type?

How to Structure Your Answer:

1. Mention the key classification criteria
2. Describe each type briefly
3. Add examples for clarity

Sample Answer: "Embedded systems can be classified in several ways depending on different criteria:

1. Based on Performance and Functional Requirements:

- **Real-Time Embedded Systems:** Designed to perform tasks within strict timing constraints (e.g., anti-lock braking systems, industrial controllers).
- **Standalone Embedded Systems:** Operate independently without relying on a host system (e.g., digital cameras, MP3 players).
- **Networked Embedded Systems:** Communicate with other systems via wired or wireless networks (e.g., smart home devices, IoT sensors).
- **Mobile Embedded Systems:** Found in portable devices (e.g., smartphones, GPS devices).

2. Based on Complexity:

- **Small-Scale Embedded Systems:** Use 8- or 16-bit microcontrollers, simple software (e.g., automatic door controllers).
- **Medium-Scale Embedded Systems:** Use more powerful processors and real-time operating systems (e.g., vending machines, washing machines).
- **Sophisticated Embedded Systems:** Complex hardware and software with multiple processors (e.g., aircraft control systems, robotics).

3. Based on Application Domain:
- **Consumer Electronics:** TVs, smartwatches
- **Automotive:** Cruise control, airbags
- **Medical Devices:** Heart rate monitors, infusion pumps
- **Industrial:** PLCs, SCADA systems

Each classification highlights how embedded systems differ in terms of application, scale, and processing needs."

Do and Don't Section

Do:

- ✓ Use structured categories
- ✓ Give clear examples for each class
- ✓ Explain classification logic briefly

Don't:

- ✗ Overload with unnecessary technical jargon
- ✗ Mix classification criteria without explanation
- ✗ Skip practical examples

Beginner Tip: Start by identifying what a system does and how complex it is — this usually points to its classification.

Final Thought: A strong answer shows not just memorization but comprehension. Classifying embedded systems helps you communicate more precisely about design needs and system behavior.

Interview Question 6: What Is a Real-Time System in the Embedded Context?

Why This Question Is Asked: Understanding real-time systems is critical in embedded roles, especially where timing is crucial. This question evaluates your grasp of real-time concepts and their practical implications in embedded design.

What the Interviewer Wants to Know:

- Do you understand the definition of a real-time system?
- Can you distinguish between hard and soft real-time systems?
- Can you relate real-time behavior to real-world use cases?

How to Structure Your Answer:

1. Define a real-time system
2. Differentiate between hard and soft real-time systems
3. Provide practical examples
4. Mention real-time operating systems (RTOS) if applicable

Sample Answer: "A real-time system is an embedded system that responds to inputs or events within a guaranteed time constraint. The correctness of the system depends not only on the logical result but also on the time it takes to deliver that result.

Types of Real-Time Systems:

- **Hard Real-Time Systems:** Missing a deadline can lead to catastrophic failure. Examples: Airbag deployment systems, pacemakers, industrial control systems.
- **Soft Real-Time Systems:** Missing a deadline is undesirable but not disastrous. Examples: Streaming audio/video, online transaction systems.

Real-time systems often use a Real-Time Operating System (RTOS) to manage task scheduling and ensure timely responses. RTOS ensures deterministic task execution, which is essential for time-sensitive applications."

Do and Don't Section

Do:

- ✓ Clearly define what a real-time system is
- ✓ Differentiate between hard and soft real-time categories
- ✓ Give strong real-world examples

Don't:

- ✗ Confuse real-time with high performance or fast systems
- ✗ Forget to mention timing constraints
- ✗ Provide only abstract definitions without examples

Beginner Tip: A microwave oven timer is not real-time — it can be delayed. But an airbag system in a car must react instantly. That's the difference between general and real-time response.

Final Thought: Real-time systems are essential where timing determines safety or reliability. A clear understanding of this concept shows your readiness to work on mission-critical embedded projects.

Interview Question 7: What Is the Difference Between Hard Real-Time and Soft Real-Time Systems?

Why This Question Is Asked: This question tests your ability to distinguish between two fundamental types of real-time systems. It's crucial in embedded development, especially for safety-critical applications.

What the Interviewer Wants to Know:

- Do you understand what makes a system 'hard' or 'soft' real-time?
- Can you explain the consequences of timing failures?
- Can you give relevant examples?

How to Structure Your Answer:

1. Define both hard and soft real-time systems
2. Compare them based on critical factors (e.g., timing, consequences of delay)
3. Provide real-world examples
4. Use a table for clarity if needed

Sample Answer: "The key difference between hard and soft real-time systems lies in how strictly they adhere to timing deadlines.

Hard Real-Time Systems: These systems must meet all deadlines, no exceptions. Failing to respond within the time constraint can cause system failure or even put lives at risk.

Soft Real-Time Systems: These systems aim to meet deadlines but can tolerate occasional delays. Missing a deadline may degrade performance but won't cause critical failure.

Comparison Table:

Aspect	Hard Real-Time System	Soft Real-Time System
Deadline Tolerance	No tolerance for missed deadlines	Some tolerance for missed deadlines
Consequence of Failure	Catastrophic (safety, security risk)	Reduced performance, no major harm
Predictability	Highly predictable and deterministic	Less predictable, may adapt dynamically
Examples	Pacemakers, airbag systems, flight control	Streaming services, online games

Do and Don't Section

Do:

- ✓ Use a table for clear comparison
- ✓ Emphasize timing and consequences
- ✓ Relate to real-life examples

Don't:

- ✗ Mix up terms like 'fast' with 'real-time'
- ✗ Forget to explain implications of delays
- ✗ Provide definitions without contrast

Beginner Tip: Think: Would a missed deadline cause failure or just inconvenience? That's your clue.

Final Thought: Understanding this distinction shows your ability to design and assess systems based on reliability and timing sensitivity — essential in embedded roles.

Interview Question 8: What Is a Microcontroller?

Why This Question Is Asked: This foundational question checks your basic understanding of embedded system components. A strong answer shows that you grasp how microcontrollers serve as the core of most embedded devices.

What the Interviewer Wants to Know:

- Do you understand the definition and role of a microcontroller?
- Can you differentiate it from a microprocessor?
- Are you aware of its components and uses?

How to Structure Your Answer:

1. Define what a microcontroller is
2. Mention its internal components
3. Explain its purpose and typical applications

Sample Answer: "A microcontroller is a compact integrated circuit designed to perform specific operations in embedded systems. It contains a processor core, memory (RAM and ROM), and input/output peripherals all on a single chip.

Microcontrollers are optimized for controlling tasks such as reading sensors, toggling outputs, or communicating with other devices. They are used in applications like home appliances, cars, industrial machines, and IoT devices.

Unlike general-purpose microprocessors, which require external components for memory and I/O, microcontrollers are self-contained, making them ideal for dedicated, low-power tasks."

Key Internal Components:

- **CPU (Central Processing Unit)** – Executes program instructions
- **Flash Memory (ROM)** – Stores the firmware or program
- **SRAM (RAM)** – Temporary storage for variables and operations

- **Timers/Counters** – Track time or generate delays
- **I/O Ports** – Communicate with sensors and actuators
- **Communication Interfaces** – UART, SPI, I2C, etc.

Do and Don't Section

Do:

- ✓ Define it in simple terms
- ✓ Mention all key internal blocks
- ✓ Relate it to practical devices

Don't:

- ✗ Confuse it with a general-purpose computer
- ✗ Leave out its integrated nature
- ✗ Use too much jargon for a basic concept

Beginner Tip: Explore development boards like Arduino or STM32. They give hands-on experience with how microcontrollers operate and interact with the real world.

Final Thought: This is a core concept in embedded systems. A clear and confident explanation of microcontrollers shows you're well-grounded in hardware basics.

Interview Question 9: What Is a Microprocessor?

Why This Question Is Asked: This question evaluates your understanding of one of the fundamental components in computing systems. It's often asked to see if you can differentiate between microprocessors and microcontrollers.

What the Interviewer Wants to Know:
- Do you know what a microprocessor is?
- Can you explain how it differs from a microcontroller?
- Are you aware of its typical applications and structure?

How to Structure Your Answer:

1. Define what a microprocessor is
2. Describe its architecture and key components
3. Contrast it with a microcontroller
4. Provide real-world examples

Sample Answer: "A microprocessor is an integrated circuit (IC) that contains only the central processing unit (CPU) of a computer. It is the brain of general-purpose computing systems, responsible for executing instructions and processing data.

Unlike a microcontroller, a microprocessor does not include internal memory (RAM, ROM) or input/output peripherals on the same chip. These must be connected externally, allowing greater flexibility but also increasing complexity, power consumption, and cost.

Microprocessors are used in devices that require high computational power and multitasking, such as personal computers, laptops, and servers."

Key Characteristics:

- **CPU Only:** Focused on high-speed data processing
- **External Components:** Requires external RAM, ROM, I/O interfaces
- **Higher Performance:** Supports multitasking and complex OS like Windows or Linux
- **Examples:** Intel Core i7, AMD Ryzen, ARM Cortex-A processors

Difference from Microcontroller:

- Microprocessor: General-purpose, powerful, needs external components
- Microcontroller: All-in-one, task-specific, low power

Do and Don't Section

Do:

- ✓ Explain the structure clearly
- ✓ Contrast with microcontroller if asked
- ✓ Give examples of typical devices

Don't:

- ✗ Confuse it with embedded applications (unless it's a high-end embedded system)
- ✗ Omit the need for external peripherals
- ✗ Assume the interviewer knows the distinction

Beginner Tip: Think of a desktop CPU — it's a microprocessor. Now think of a washing machine controller — that's usually a microcontroller.

Final Thought: Understanding microprocessors is key to grasping how general-purpose computers work. A precise, structured answer will show your depth of knowledge in computing systems.

Interview Question 10: How Is a Microcontroller Different from a Microprocessor?

Why This Question Is Asked: This is a common comparison question in embedded system interviews. It checks whether you understand the architectural and functional differences between two key processing units.

What the Interviewer Wants to Know:

- Can you distinguish between the two accurately?
- Do you understand their use cases and limitations?
- Can you explain which is better suited for embedded systems?

How to Structure Your Answer:

1. Define both terms briefly
2. Highlight key differences using a comparison format
3. Provide examples and applications

Sample Answer: "A microcontroller is a compact integrated circuit that includes a CPU, memory (RAM and ROM), and I/O peripherals all on one chip. It is designed for specific control applications such as in washing machines or traffic lights.

A microprocessor, on the other hand, contains only the CPU on a single chip. It requires external memory and I/O components to function. Microprocessors are typically used in applications requiring high processing power, like desktops and laptops."

Comparison Table:

Feature	Microcontroller	Microprocessor
Integration	Includes CPU, RAM, ROM, I/O on one chip	Only CPU; needs external memory/I/O
Application	Task-specific (e.g., embedded systems)	General-purpose computing
Cost and Power	Low cost, low power consumption	Higher cost, higher power usage
Complexity	Simple design	Complex design
Speed & Performance	Sufficient for dedicated tasks	High performance for multitasking
Examples	Arduino (ATmega328), STM32	Intel i5, ARM Cortex-A72

Do and Don't Section

Do:

- ✓ Use simple language with technical clarity
- ✓ Mention integration and application-based differences
- ✓ Support with practical examples

Don't:

- ✗ Confuse embedded use cases with general computing
- ✗ Ignore key structural differences
- ✗ Use overly vague terms like 'fast' without context

Beginner Tip: If it's a complete system on a chip and controls a device — it's a microcontroller. If it's the central unit of a computer system — it's a microprocessor.

Final Thought: Knowing the difference is critical in hardware design decisions. Your answer should show that you not only understand the theory but also the practical implications of choosing one over the other.

Interview Question 11: What Is the Role of RAM and ROM in Embedded Systems?

Why This Question Is Asked: This question evaluates your understanding of memory management in embedded systems. It's essential to know how different types of memory are used and what roles they play in system functionality.

What the Interviewer Wants to Know:

- Do you understand the function of RAM and ROM?
- Can you explain how each is used in embedded systems?
- Do you know why both are important?

How to Structure Your Answer:

1. Define RAM and ROM
2. Explain the role of each in embedded systems
3. Provide examples of their use
4. Highlight differences and why both are necessary

Sample Answer: "In embedded systems, both RAM and ROM play crucial roles in storing and managing data and instructions.

ROM (Read-Only Memory): ROM stores the firmware — the permanent software programmed into the system. It holds the instructions that run when the system is powered on. ROM is non-volatile, meaning it retains its data even when the power is off. Examples include Flash memory in microcontrollers, which stores the main program.

RAM (Random Access Memory): RAM is used for temporary data storage while the system is running. It stores variables, intermediate calculations, and stack data. RAM is volatile, meaning all data is lost when power is removed. It allows fast read/write access, essential for real-time data processing.

Together, ROM ensures the system knows what to do, while RAM helps it perform those actions during operation."

Comparison Table:

Feature	ROM	RAM
Volatility	Non-volatile	Volatile
Purpose	Stores firmware/permanent program code	Temporary data storage during runtime
Writable?	Not during normal operation	Yes, read/write at runtime
Speed	Slower	Faster
Examples	Flash memory in microcontrollers	SRAM/DRAM in embedded boards

Do and Don't Section

Do:

- ✓ Clearly define and differentiate RAM and ROM
- ✓ Mention volatility and usage
- ✓ Relate them to real embedded systems

Don't:

- ✗ Confuse their roles or characteristics
- ✗ Skip giving examples
- ✗ Use generic computer terms without embedded context

Beginner Tip: Think of ROM as the brain's long-term memory (what it always remembers), and RAM as the short-term memory used while working.

Final Thought: Memory architecture is central to embedded system performance and reliability. A solid understanding of RAM and ROM roles shows that you can design and debug systems effectively.

Interview Question 12: What Is Firmware?

Why This Question Is Asked: This question helps interviewers assess your understanding of how software integrates with hardware in embedded systems. Firmware is a key concept in system-level design and development.

What the Interviewer Wants to Know:

- Do you know what firmware is and how it differs from regular software?
- Can you explain its role in embedded systems?
- Are you aware of how and where it is stored?

How to Structure Your Answer:

1. Define what firmware is
2. Explain its function and characteristics
3. Mention how it differs from application software
4. Give examples in real-world systems

Sample Answer: "Firmware is a type of low-level software that is permanently stored in the read-only memory (ROM) or flash memory of an embedded system. It provides the necessary instructions for how the device communicates with other hardware and performs basic functions.

Firmware acts as the intermediary between the hardware and higher-level software. It is usually written in low-level languages like C or assembly and is optimized for the specific hardware it controls. Unlike regular software, firmware does not change frequently and is designed to be stable and reliable.

Examples include the BIOS in a computer, the program running on a microcontroller in a washing machine, or the firmware controlling a smart bulb."

Key Characteristics of Firmware:

- **Non-volatile:** Stored in ROM or Flash; persists after power-off
- **Hardware-specific:** Tailored to work with specific hardware
- **Stable and reliable:** Not updated frequently
- **Low-level:** Interfaces directly with hardware

Firmware vs. Application Software:

- Firmware is tightly coupled with the hardware
- Application software is user-facing and runs on top of an OS or firmware

Do and Don't Section

Do:

- ✓ Define it clearly and concisely
- ✓ Explain where and how it's used
- ✓ Include practical examples

Don't:

- ✗ Confuse it with general application software
- ✗ Forget to mention its role in hardware operation
- ✗ Ignore its storage location (ROM/Flash)

Beginner Tip: Firmware is like the built-in brain of a device — it runs the moment it's powered on and ensures everything works as it should.

Final Thought: A good understanding of firmware shows that you know how embedded systems are brought to life and controlled. It's a bridge between hardware and software that ensures the system functions correctly.

Interview Question 13: Define an Interrupt and Its Types

Why This Question Is Asked: Interrupts are central to embedded systems and real-time operations. This question tests your knowledge of how systems handle asynchronous events efficiently.

What the Interviewer Wants to Know:

- Can you define what an interrupt is?
- Do you understand the different types of interrupts?
- Can you explain how interrupts improve system responsiveness?

How to Structure Your Answer:

1. Define what an interrupt is
2. Explain why interrupts are used
3. Describe the main types of interrupts
4. Provide examples or use cases

Sample Answer: "An interrupt is a signal to the processor indicating that an immediate attention is required by an external or internal event. It temporarily halts the current program execution, saves its state, and executes a function called an Interrupt Service Routine (ISR) to handle the event.

Interrupts are crucial in embedded systems for handling real-time tasks, improving efficiency by avoiding constant polling."

Types of Interrupts:

1. **Hardware Interrupts:**
    a. Generated by external hardware devices (e.g., timers, keyboards, sensors)
    b. Example: A temperature sensor triggers an interrupt when a threshold is crossed
2. **Software Interrupts:**
    a. Triggered by software instructions (e.g., system calls or exceptions)
    b. Example: A program may invoke a software interrupt to switch to kernel mode
3. **Maskable Interrupts (IRQ):**
    a. Can be disabled or masked by the processor
    b. Used for general tasks like communication or timer events
4. **Non-Maskable Interrupts (NMI):**
    a. Cannot be disabled
    b. Used for critical events such as power failures or memory corruption
5. **Vectored Interrupts:**
    a. The address of the ISR is known beforehand and mapped
    b. Faster because of direct jumping
6. **Non-Vectored Interrupts:**
    a. The address of the ISR must be determined by polling or checking status

Do and Don't Section

Do:

- ✓ Use real-world examples
- ✓ Mention ISR and its role
- ✓ Explain the benefit of interrupts vs. polling

Don't:

- ✗ Confuse types (e.g., masking with software interrupt)
- ✗ Skip the role of ISR
- ✗ Be overly theoretical — relate to embedded systems

Beginner Tip: Imagine you're reading a book (main program), and someone rings the doorbell (interrupt). You mark your page, attend the door (ISR), then return and resume reading from where you left off.

Final Thought: Mastering interrupts is key for building responsive, efficient embedded systems. A good explanation shows you're ready to handle real-time design challenges.

Interview Question 14: What Is Interrupt Latency?

Why This Question Is Asked: Understanding interrupt latency is vital for designing real-time and responsive embedded systems. This question assesses your grasp of performance metrics in handling asynchronous events.

What the Interviewer Wants to Know:

- Do you understand the concept of latency in interrupts?
- Can you explain the factors affecting it?
- Can you suggest ways to reduce it in embedded systems?

How to Structure Your Answer:

1. Define interrupt latency
2. Mention causes and contributing factors
3. Discuss its importance in real-time systems
4. Describe ways to minimize it

Sample Answer: "Interrupt latency is the time delay between the occurrence of an interrupt request and the execution of the first instruction of the corresponding Interrupt Service Routine (ISR). It is a critical parameter in real-time systems where timely response to events is essential.

Low interrupt latency ensures fast reaction to events such as sensor inputs, communication signals, or user actions."

Factors Affecting Interrupt Latency:

- **Processor speed and architecture**
- **Interrupt prioritization mechanism**
- **Number of active interrupts**
- **Interrupt masking or disabling in software**
- **Length of the currently executing instruction or ISR**

Importance in Embedded Systems:

- Critical in safety systems (e.g., airbags, medical devices)
- Affects overall system responsiveness and real-time performance

Ways to Reduce Interrupt Latency:

- Use fast processors or real-time cores
- Optimize ISR routines to be short and efficient
- Avoid disabling interrupts for extended periods
- Use hardware priority levels for interrupts
- Minimize use of nested interrupts

Do and Don't Section

Do:

- ✓ Define latency precisely
- ✓ Explain why it matters in embedded systems
- ✓ Mention optimization strategies

Don't:

- ✗ Confuse it with ISR execution time (they are different)
- ✗ Overlook hardware and software factors
- ✗ Ignore real-world implications

Beginner Tip: Think of it like answering a phone call — the time from the ring (interrupt) to saying "Hello" (first ISR instruction) is your latency.

Final Thought: Interrupt latency is a crucial performance indicator in embedded and real-time systems. Understanding and minimizing it shows your skill in designing responsive and reliable systems.

Interview Question 15: What Are Polling and Interrupt-Driven I/O?

Why This Question Is Asked: This question helps interviewers evaluate your understanding of two key I/O handling methods in embedded systems — polling and interrupt-driven I/O. Your answer should reflect your awareness of how I/O events are detected and managed efficiently.

What the Interviewer Wants to Know:

- Can you define and differentiate polling and interrupt-driven I/O?
- Do you understand their advantages and disadvantages?
- Can you explain when to use each method?

How to Structure Your Answer:

1. Define polling
2. Define interrupt-driven I/O
3. Compare them based on responsiveness, efficiency, and complexity
4. Give real-world examples or use cases

Sample Answer: "Polling and interrupt-driven I/O are two methods for handling input/output events in embedded systems.

Polling: In polling, the processor repeatedly checks the status of a peripheral to see if it needs attention. This is done in a loop, consuming CPU cycles regardless of whether an event occurs.

- **Example:** A microcontroller checking a button press in every loop iteration.

Interrupt-Driven I/O: In this method, the processor continues with other tasks until an I/O event occurs. The peripheral sends an interrupt signal to the processor, which then pauses its current task, executes the corresponding ISR, and resumes the original task.

- **Example:** A UART interrupt that triggers when new serial data arrives.

Comparison Table:

Aspect	Polling	Interrupt-Driven I/O
CPU Utilization	High (busy-waiting)	Low (CPU free until needed)
Efficiency	Less efficient	More efficient
Responsiveness	May miss events if not fast enough	Immediate response
Complexity	Simple implementation	More complex (requires ISR and setup)
Use Case	Simple or periodic tasks	Time-critical or sporadic events

Do and Don't Section

Do:

- ✓ Clearly define and differentiate both methods
- ✓ Mention use cases and efficiency trade-offs
- ✓ Use real-world examples

Don't:

- ✗ Confuse polling with delay-based loops
- ✗ Ignore CPU usage differences
- ✗ Forget the importance of ISR in interrupt-based I/O

Beginner Tip: If your system needs to react immediately to inputs (e.g., a door alarm), use interrupts. If it's okay to check occasionally (e.g., battery level), polling might suffice.

Final Thought: Choosing between polling and interrupts depends on system requirements. A good answer reflects your ability to balance performance, responsiveness, and simplicity in I/O design.

Interview Question 16: What Is the Bootloader in Embedded Systems?

Why This Question Is Asked: Interviewers ask this question to evaluate your knowledge of system startup processes and memory initialization. A solid understanding of the bootloader shows your ability to manage low-level system tasks.

What the Interviewer Wants to Know:

- Do you understand what a bootloader is and its purpose?
- Can you explain how it works in embedded systems?
- Are you aware of its role in firmware updating and system initialization?

How to Structure Your Answer:

1. Define what a bootloader is
2. Explain its role and how it functions
3. Mention its importance in firmware development and updates
4. Provide real-world examples

Sample Answer: "A bootloader is a small program that runs immediately after a device is powered on or reset. It initializes the hardware, sets up the environment, and then loads the main firmware or operating system into memory to begin execution.

In embedded systems, the bootloader typically resides in a protected section of flash memory and ensures that the system starts correctly. It can also support in-field firmware updates, often via UART, USB, or network protocols like TFTP or OTA (Over-the-Air).

For example, in STM32 microcontrollers, the built-in bootloader can receive firmware via serial or USB interfaces, making it useful for remote or initial programming."

Key Functions of a Bootloader:

*   Hardware initialization (e.g., clock setup, memory config)
*   Verification of the main application image (e.g., checksum, signature)
*   Loading the main application code into RAM or starting it from Flash
*   Supporting firmware updates

Do and Don't Section

Do:

*   ✓ Define the bootloader clearly and concisely
*   ✓ Explain both its startup and update functionalities
*   ✓ Mention protected memory and security considerations

Don't:

- ✗ Confuse it with the main application firmware
- ✗ Forget to mention startup sequence and initialization
- ✗ Overlook its role in update mechanisms

Beginner Tip: Think of a bootloader as the ignition system in a car — it starts the engine (main firmware) and checks that everything is ready before handing over control.

Final Thought: The bootloader is a critical component in embedded systems for managing reliable startup and firmware upgrades. Understanding it shows your readiness to handle low-level system tasks and lifecycle management.

Interview Question 17: What Is an Embedded Operating System?

Why This Question Is Asked: This question assesses your understanding of how operating systems work within resource-constrained environments. Knowing about embedded OSes is essential for candidates involved in real-time or complex embedded applications.

What the Interviewer Wants to Know:

- Do you know what an embedded operating system is?
- Can you explain how it differs from general-purpose OSes?
- Are you aware of examples and their use cases?

How to Structure Your Answer:

1. Define what an embedded operating system is
2. Explain key features and limitations
3. Compare with general-purpose OSes
4. Provide real-world examples

Sample Answer: "An embedded operating system is a specialized operating system designed to run on embedded systems — devices that perform specific functions within a larger system. These OSes manage hardware resources, provide real-time capabilities, and often have a smaller footprint than general-purpose operating systems.

They are optimized for reliability, speed, and efficient memory usage in devices like routers, automotive control units, and industrial controllers. Some embedded OSes include real-time features for deterministic task execution."

Key Features of Embedded Operating Systems:

- Small memory footprint
- Fast and deterministic task scheduling
- Limited or no user interface
- Real-time support (for RTOS)
- High reliability and stability

Examples of Embedded OSes:

- FreeRTOS
- VxWorks
- Zephyr OS
- µC/OS-II or µC/OS-III
- Embedded Linux (e.g., Yocto, Buildroot)

Comparison with General-Purpose OS:

- Embedded OS: Resource-constrained, task-specific, real-time capable
- General-purpose OS: Feature-rich, multitasking, used in PCs and servers

Do and Don't Section

Do:

- ✅ Mention the purpose and features of embedded OSes
- ✅ Provide examples and use cases
- ✅ Highlight real-time capabilities if relevant

Don't:

- ❌ Confuse embedded OS with just small versions of desktop OSes
- ❌ Skip discussing performance or memory constraints
- ❌ Overlook reliability and uptime requirements

Beginner Tip: Think of a smartwatch or a home router — they run embedded operating systems that are designed for their specific jobs.

Final Thought: An embedded OS is essential for managing complex devices with strict performance and reliability needs. Understanding its role shows your ability to work on both software and system-level design in embedded environments.

Interview Question 18: What Is Bare-Metal Programming?

Why This Question Is Asked: Bare-metal programming is a core concept in embedded system development. Interviewers ask this to gauge your experience working close to the hardware without the aid of an operating system.

What the Interviewer Wants to Know:

- Do you understand what bare-metal programming means?
- Can you explain its advantages and limitations?
- Are you familiar with typical use cases and environments?

How to Structure Your Answer:

1. Define bare-metal programming
2. Explain how it differs from OS-based programming
3. Highlight pros and cons
4. Provide examples and relevant use cases

Sample Answer: "Bare-metal programming refers to writing software that runs directly on the hardware without an operating system. The developer manually manages all hardware resources such as timers, interrupts, and peripherals.

This approach is common in small, resource-constrained embedded systems where performance, determinism, and minimal overhead are critical. It's often used for microcontrollers like the STM32, AVR, or PIC."

Key Characteristics of Bare-Metal Programming:

- No operating system or kernel
- Direct register-level hardware access
- Developers write initialization and control routines for peripherals
- Typically written in C or assembly

Advantages:

- Low latency and high performance
- Full control over hardware
- Lower memory and power usage

Disadvantages:

- More complex and error-prone development
- Harder to scale or maintain
- Lacks built-in scheduling and abstraction

Use Cases:

- Industrial control systems
- Simple IoT devices
- Safety-critical systems (e.g., automotive ECUs, medical devices)

Do and Don't Section

Do:

- ✓ Define it with clarity and focus
- ✓ Mention the benefits and when to use it
- ✓ Provide real-world microcontroller examples

Don't:

- ✗ Confuse it with minimal OS environments
- ✗ Skip hardware control or peripheral handling
- ✗ Ignore its relevance in real-time or safety-critical systems

Beginner Tip: If you're blinking an LED on an STM32 or Arduino without an RTOS or OS, you're doing bare-metal programming.

Final Thought: Bare-metal programming is foundational in embedded development. Mastery of it shows your ability to handle low-level software design, optimize performance, and manage resources directly.

Interview Question 19: What Are Timers and Counters?

Why This Question Is Asked: Timers and counters are essential hardware features in embedded systems. Interviewers use this question to evaluate your understanding of how microcontrollers handle time-related operations and event counting.

What the Interviewer Wants to Know:

- Do you understand the difference between timers and counters?
- Can you explain their function in embedded systems?
- Are you aware of typical use cases?

How to Structure Your Answer:

1. Define what a timer is
2. Define what a counter is
3. Explain the difference and how they work
4. Provide examples of their use in real-world applications

Sample Answer: "Timers and counters are peripherals in microcontrollers that increment or decrement a register value based on specific input signals.

Timer: A timer increments based on an internal clock source. It is commonly used to measure time intervals, generate delays, or trigger periodic events (like blinking LEDs or generating PWM signals).

Counter: A counter increments based on external events or signals, such as the number of pulses received from a sensor. It is useful for event counting or frequency measurement.

Most modern microcontrollers allow the same hardware peripheral to operate either as a timer or a counter depending on the configuration."

Comparison Table:

Aspect	Timer	Counter
Source	Internal clock	External signal or pulse
Use Case	Delays, time measurement, PWM	Event counting, external pulse monitoring
Example	LED blinking every 1s	Counting button presses
Configur ation	Typically time-based interrupts	Triggered by external events

Do and Don't Section

Do:

- ✓ Define both with clarity
- ✓ Use examples to show real use cases
- ✓ Highlight clock source differences

Don't:

- ✗ Assume they are always separate peripherals (they often share hardware)
- ✗ Mix up internal vs. external signal sources
- ✗ Skip practical application contexts

Beginner Tip: If you're using a delay function in Arduino like `delay(1000)`, a timer is working behind the scenes. If you're counting how many times a pin goes HIGH, that's a counter.

Final Thought: Timers and counters are foundational in embedded system design. Clear understanding and configuration of these modules allow you to build accurate and efficient applications.

Interview Question 20: What Is a Watchdog Timer?

Why This Question Is Asked: This question tests your understanding of system reliability and fault recovery in embedded systems. The watchdog timer is a key feature for ensuring systems recover from unexpected failures.

What the Interviewer Wants to Know:

- Do you understand the purpose of a watchdog timer?
- Can you explain how it works?
- Are you aware of how it enhances system reliability?

How to Structure Your Answer:

1. Define what a watchdog timer is
2. Explain how it operates
3. Describe typical use cases
4. Mention advantages and precautions

Sample Answer: "A watchdog timer is a hardware timer used in embedded systems to detect and recover from software malfunctions. It operates by requiring the system to periodically reset the timer (often called 'kicking' or 'feeding' the watchdog).

If the timer is not reset within a specified time window — usually due to a software hang, crash, or infinite loop — it assumes the system is unresponsive and initiates a system reset or other corrective action.

This mechanism ensures that the system does not stay stuck in an error state indefinitely."

How It Works:

- The application periodically resets the watchdog timer
- If the timer reaches its limit without being reset, it triggers a system reset
- Often used in safety-critical and unattended systems

Use Cases:

- Industrial control systems
- Automotive ECUs
- Remote sensors and IoT devices
- Medical equipment

Benefits:

- Increases system reliability
- Automatically recovers from software faults
- Prevents system hangs

Precautions:

- Avoid improper use (e.g., resetting the watchdog in the wrong place can mask errors)
- Test thoroughly to ensure watchdog behavior is predictable and safe

Do and Don't Section

Do:

- ✓ Clearly define and explain the purpose
- ✓ Include examples of systems where it's critical
- ✓ Mention best practices for implementation

Don't:

- ✗ Confuse it with other types of timers
- ✗ Forget to mention the importance of regular resetting
- ✗ Ignore the impact of improper configuration

Beginner Tip: Think of a watchdog timer like a supervisor — if it doesn't hear back from the worker (software) in time, it assumes there's a problem and restarts the work.

Final Thought: The watchdog timer is a vital safeguard for embedded systems. Understanding it reflects your ability to design reliable, fault-tolerant applications.

Interview Question 21: What Is an ADC? How Is It Used?

Why This Question Is Asked: Interviewers ask this to assess your understanding of interfacing analog signals with digital systems. ADCs (Analog-to-Digital Converters) are essential in embedded systems that need to process real-world analog data.

What the Interviewer Wants to Know:

- Do you understand what an ADC does?
- Can you explain its role in converting analog signals to digital?
- Are you familiar with how it's used in embedded systems?

How to Structure Your Answer:

1. Define what an ADC is
2. Explain its working principle
3. Describe its use in embedded systems
4. Give practical examples

Sample Answer: "An ADC, or Analog-to-Digital Converter, is a device or circuit that converts continuous analog signals into discrete digital values. This allows microcontrollers, which operate in the digital domain, to read and process real-world analog inputs such as temperature, light, or voltage levels.

The ADC samples the analog signal at specific intervals and converts each sample into a binary value based on its voltage level and the resolution of the ADC (e.g., 8-bit, 10-bit, 12-bit)."

How It Is Used in Embedded Systems:

- Sensors (e.g., temperature, pressure, light) output analog signals
- The microcontroller's built-in ADC reads these signals and converts them into digital values
- These digital values are then used in software for control, monitoring, or display

Example Applications:

- Measuring temperature with LM35 sensor
- Reading potentiometer values for user input
- Monitoring battery voltage in a power system

Key Terms:

- **Resolution:** Number of bits (e.g., 10-bit ADC gives values from 0 to 1023)
- **Sampling Rate:** How often the ADC samples the signal
- **Reference Voltage (Vref):** Defines the input range the ADC can read

Do and Don't Section

Do:

- ✓ Define ADC clearly
- ✓ Mention where and how it is used
- ✓ Provide sensor-based real-life examples

Don't:

- ✗ Confuse ADC with DAC (Digital-to-Analog Converter)
- ✗ Forget to mention resolution or sampling concepts
- ✗ Skip explaining its practical importance

Beginner Tip: If you're using a temperature sensor on an Arduino and calling `analogRead()`, you're using the built-in ADC to convert voltage into digital values.

Final Thought: ADCs are a bridge between the analog world and digital processing. A solid understanding of how they work and where they're used is key for any embedded system developer.

Interview Question 22: What Is a DAC? Give an Application Example

Why This Question Is Asked: DACs (Digital-to-Analog Converters) are used when digital systems need to generate real-world analog outputs. Understanding this shows your grasp of signal generation and control in embedded systems.

What the Interviewer Wants to Know:

- Do you know what a DAC is?
- Can you explain how it's used and where it fits in?
- Are you familiar with real-life examples?

How to Structure Your Answer:

1. Define a DAC
2. Explain its working principle
3. Give practical application examples
4. Mention importance in system design

Sample Answer: "A DAC (Digital-to-Analog Converter) is a device that converts digital numeric data into a continuous analog voltage or current. It's the reverse of an ADC and is used when a system needs to output real-world signals such as sound, voltage control, or analog waveform generation."

Application Example:

- In audio systems, a DAC converts digital audio data into analog signals to drive headphones or speakers.

Other Use Cases:

- Signal generation in waveform generators (sine, triangle, square waves)
- Analog voltage output to control motors or actuators
- Dimming LEDs smoothly using analog voltage instead of PWM

Do and Don't Section

Do:

- ✓ Clearly define what a DAC is
- ✓ Mention real and relatable application examples
- ✓ Explain the role of DAC in bridging digital and analog domains

Don't:

- ✕ Confuse DAC with ADC
- ✕ Forget to mention why analog output is needed
- ✕ Be vague about its application

Beginner Tip: Think of a DAC as a translator that takes digital instructions and turns them into smooth, real-world signals — like music playing from your phone.

Final Thought: Understanding DACs is crucial for designing systems that interact with the physical world. They are key in audio, control, and analog output applications.

Interview Question 23: What Are GPIO Pins?

Why This Question Is Asked: GPIOs (General-Purpose Input/Output) are foundational to embedded hardware control. This question checks your practical knowledge of how microcontrollers interact with the external world.

What the Interviewer Wants to Know:

- Do you understand what GPIO pins are and how they function?
- Can you differentiate between input and output configurations?
- Are you familiar with practical applications?

How to Structure Your Answer:

1. Define what GPIO pins are
2. Explain input vs. output mode
3. Give common examples of GPIO usage
4. Mention configuration and control methods

Sample Answer: "GPIO (General-Purpose Input/Output) pins are flexible digital pins on a microcontroller or processor that can be configured either as input or output to interact with external components.

In input mode, they can read signals like button presses or sensor outputs. In output mode, they can drive LEDs, relays, or send digital signals to other components. GPIOs are configured and controlled through software, typically using registers or abstraction layers in embedded frameworks."

Key GPIO Modes:

- **Input Mode:** Reads external signals (e.g., button, sensor)
- **Output Mode:** Sends digital signals (e.g., LED ON/OFF)
- **Pull-up/Pull-down:** Used in input mode to define default state
- **Interrupt-on-change:** Used to detect events without polling

Common Applications:

- Blinking LEDs
- Reading button or switch states
- Driving relays and buzzers
- Interfacing with shift registers or LCDs

Do and Don't Section

Do:

- ✓ Define GPIO clearly
- ✓ Differentiate between input and output use cases
- ✓ Provide real-world examples

Don't:

- ✗ Confuse GPIOs with analog pins or dedicated peripherals
- ✗ Skip discussing software configuration
- ✗ Be vague about usage scenarios

Beginner Tip: Blinking an LED or detecting a button press is often the first hands-on experiment with GPIOs — it's the starting point of learning embedded systems.

Final Thought: Understanding GPIO pins is essential for interfacing embedded systems with the real world. Mastery of GPIOs reflects your foundational knowledge in hardware control and embedded programming.

Interview Question 24: Explain the Difference Between Volatile and Non-Volatile Memory

Why This Question Is Asked: Understanding memory types is crucial for efficient and reliable embedded system design. This question checks your knowledge of how data is stored and preserved in embedded applications.

What the Interviewer Wants to Know:

- Do you understand what volatile and non-volatile memory are?
- Can you differentiate between them clearly?
- Are you aware of where each type is used in embedded systems?

How to Structure Your Answer:

1. Define volatile and non-volatile memory
2. Highlight key differences
3. Provide examples of each
4. Explain their roles in embedded systems

Sample Answer: "Volatile memory loses its content when the power is turned off, while non-volatile memory retains data even without power.
Volatile Memory:
- Used for temporary data storage
- Requires continuous power to maintain information
- Fast access speeds
- Example: RAM (Random Access Memory)

Non-Volatile Memory:

- Retains data after power loss
- Used for firmware, configurations, and logs
- Slower than RAM but permanent
- Example: ROM, Flash memory, EEPROM

In embedded systems, volatile memory is used for runtime operations and variable storage, while non-volatile memory holds program code (firmware) and persistent settings."

Comparison Table:

Feature	Volatile Memory	Non-Volatile Memory
Power Dependence	Requires power	Retains data without power
Use Case	Runtime data, variables	Firmware, configurations
Speed	Fast	Slower than RAM
Examples	SRAM, DRAM	Flash, EEPROM, ROM

Do and Don't Section

Do:

- ✓ Define both types clearly
- ✓ Provide examples and uses
- ✓ Mention relevance to embedded systems

Don't:

- ✗ Confuse with cache or registers
- ✗ Skip practical implications like data loss
- ✗ Be vague about usage contexts

Beginner Tip: If your data disappears when the device turns off, it's stored in volatile memory. If it stays, it's in non-volatile memory.

Final Thought: The choice between volatile and non-volatile memory is crucial for designing reliable and efficient embedded systems. A good answer shows awareness of memory behavior and system design strategy.

Interview Question 25: What Is Memory-Mapped I/O?

Why This Question Is Asked: Memory-mapped I/O is a core concept in embedded systems for controlling peripherals. This question tests your understanding of how processors interact with hardware devices.

What the Interviewer Wants to Know:

- Do you understand how I/O devices are accessed in memory-mapped systems?
- Can you explain the difference between memory-mapped I/O and port-mapped I/O?
- Are you familiar with how to use memory-mapped I/O in embedded coding?

How to Structure Your Answer:

1. Define memory-mapped I/O
2. Describe how it works
3. Compare with port-mapped I/O (if relevant)
4. Provide examples in real-world use

Sample Answer: "Memory-mapped I/O is a technique in embedded systems where peripheral device registers are assigned specific addresses within the system's memory space. This allows the CPU to read from and write to peripherals using standard memory access instructions.

For example, a GPIO pin or a UART module may be controlled by writing values to specific memory addresses defined in the microcontroller's datasheet."

How It Works:

- Each peripheral is mapped to a unique memory address
- The CPU accesses I/O devices using regular memory access instructions (e.g., LDR, STR, MOV)
- Typically used in ARM Cortex-M, AVR, and other microcontroller architectures

Comparison with Port-Mapped I/O:

- **Memory-Mapped I/O:** Same instructions for memory and I/O access, more flexible
- **Port-Mapped I/O:** Uses special instructions for I/O (e.g., IN, OUT), common in older x86 systems

Example:

```
#define GPIO_PORT (*(volatile unsigned int*)0x40021000)
GPIO_PORT = 0x01;  // Set GPIO pin
```

Do and Don't Section

Do:

- ✅ Explain access through memory space
- ✅ Use a practical code example
- ✅ Mention CPU instruction reuse benefit

Don't:

- ✗ Confuse with general memory access
- ✗ Skip how it simplifies hardware access
- ✗ Overlook the hardware address mapping concept

Beginner Tip: When you set or read a pin using a specific address in your code, you're using memory-mapped I/O — it's like pretending your hardware is just part of your RAM.

Final Thought: Memory-mapped I/O simplifies embedded programming by allowing direct access to peripherals as if they were memory. A solid answer reflects your understanding of low-level hardware-software integration.

Section 2: Embedded C & Programming Concepts (26–50)

Interview Question 26: What Is Embedded C?

Why This Question Is Asked: Embedded C is the standard programming language for microcontroller-based applications. This question tests your familiarity with low-level programming in embedded systems.

What the Interviewer Wants to Know:
- Do you understand what makes Embedded C different from standard C?
- Can you explain its importance in embedded development?
- Are you familiar with the types of operations and hardware access it enables?

How to Structure Your Answer:
1. Define Embedded C
2. Explain its relationship with standard C
3. Mention unique features for embedded programming
4. Provide real-world examples

Sample Answer: "Embedded C is a set of language extensions to the C programming language designed for programming embedded systems. While it follows standard C syntax, it includes specific features and libraries to interact with hardware directly, such as setting register values, reading sensor data, or controlling I/O pins.

Embedded C is used to write firmware that runs on microcontrollers like AVR, ARM Cortex-M, or PIC. It allows direct control over memory, peripherals, and execution flow with minimal abstraction, making it ideal for performance-critical and resource-constrained applications."

Key Features of Embedded C:

- Direct hardware access using memory-mapped registers
- Bit manipulation operations
- Precise timing control
- Efficient use of memory and CPU resources

Example Use Cases:

- Writing firmware for microcontrollers (e.g., blinking LEDs, reading sensors)
- Controlling GPIOs, timers, and communication interfaces (SPI, UART, I2C)
- Developing real-time embedded applications (e.g., motor control, sensor fusion)

Beginner Tip: If you've ever programmed an Arduino using `digitalWrite()` or toggled a pin with `PORTB |= (1<<PB0);`, you're already working with Embedded C concepts.

Do and Don't Section

Do:

- ✅ Mention hardware-level interaction
- ✅ Highlight differences from desktop C programming
- ✅ Use relatable microcontroller examples

Don't:

- ✖ Confuse Embedded C with assembly or standard C
- ✖ Ignore the importance of memory and timing constraints
- ✖ Skip mentioning direct register access

Final Thought: Embedded C is the foundation of firmware development. Knowing it well shows you're equipped to build reliable, efficient embedded systems at both low and mid-level abstraction layers.

Interview Question 27: How Is Embedded C Different from Standard C?

Why This Question Is Asked: Understanding the differences between Embedded C and standard C reveals your knowledge of system-level programming, resource management, and real-time control in embedded environments.

What the Interviewer Wants to Know:

- Can you distinguish Embedded C from desktop/standard C?
- Are you familiar with the additional features and constraints of Embedded C?
- Do you understand the hardware-level capabilities it enables?

How to Structure Your Answer:

1. Define standard C and Embedded C
2. Compare their use cases
3. Highlight differences in capabilities and features
4. Provide example differences in syntax or functions

Sample Answer: "Standard C is a general-purpose programming language used primarily for desktop applications and operating systems, with standard libraries and a focus on portability and abstraction.

Embedded C is an extension of standard C used for developing firmware for microcontrollers and embedded devices. It includes additional features like direct memory and register access, bitwise operations, and hardware control. While the syntax is largely the same, Embedded C interacts directly with the hardware through special registers and memory-mapped I/O."

Comparison Table:

Aspect	Standard C	Embedded C
Target Environment	Desktop, servers, OS-level apps	Microcontrollers, embedded devices
Hardware Access	Not direct, usually abstracted	Direct via registers and memory-mapped I/O
Libraries	Standard libraries (stdio, stdlib)	Device-specific libraries (e.g., avr/io.h)
Resources Available	Abundant memory and CPU	Limited resources (RAM, Flash, CPU)
Timing Requirements	Not typically real-time	Often real-time and deterministic
Common Usage	File systems, apps, networking	LED control, sensor reading, timers, UART

Example Difference:

- **Standard C:** `printf("Hello World\n");`
- **Embedded C:** `PORTB |= (1 << PB0); // Set a GPIO pin high`

Do and Don't Section

Do:

- ✓ Compare both in terms of usage and system constraints
- ✓ Provide hardware-level interaction examples
- ✓ Emphasize timing and resource limitations in Embedded C

Don't:

- ✗ Assume they are completely different languages
- ✗ Ignore the shared syntax and core features
- ✗ Skip the context of use (desktop vs embedded)

Beginner Tip: Think of standard C as writing for a computer, and Embedded C as writing for a tiny computer inside a washing machine or a thermostat.

Final Thought: While Embedded C is based on standard C, the environment, constraints, and purpose make it a specialized skill. Understanding these differences is vital for building reliable and efficient embedded systems.

Interview Question 28: What Are Bitwise Operators?

Why This Question Is Asked: Bitwise operators are essential in embedded programming for register manipulation, masking, and setting specific bits. Interviewers use this question to assess your low-level programming skills.

What the Interviewer Wants to Know:

- Do you understand how to use bitwise operators?
- Can you explain their function and applications in embedded systems?
- Are you able to write or interpret bit-level code?

How to Structure Your Answer:

1. Define bitwise operators
2. List common bitwise operators and their functions
3. Give practical embedded examples
4. Explain why they are important

Sample Answer: "Bitwise operators are used to perform operations directly on the binary representation of integers. They are commonly used in embedded systems to manipulate specific bits in control registers, set or clear flags, and manage hardware efficiently."

Common Bitwise Operators:

- & (AND): Clears bits
- | (OR): Sets bits
- ^ (XOR): Toggles bits
- ~ (NOT): Inverts bits
- << (Left Shift): Shifts bits left (multiplies by 2)
- >> (Right Shift): Shifts bits right (divides by 2)

Practical Examples:

```
PORTB |= (1 << PB0);  // Set bit PB0 (turn ON LED)
PORTB &= ~(1 << PB0); // Clear bit PB0 (turn OFF LED)
PORTB ^= (1 << PB0);  // Toggle bit PB0
```

Why They Matter in Embedded Systems:

- Efficient memory and register manipulation
- Enables low-level hardware control
- Crucial for flag checks, state machines, and ISR optimization

Do and Don't Section

Do:

- ✅ Explain with clear binary-level intent
- ✅ Provide common examples used in embedded firmware
- ✅ Emphasize real hardware use cases

Don't:

- ✗ Use bitwise operations for unrelated tasks
- ✗ Confuse logical operators (&&, ||) with bitwise ones
- ✗ Skip explaining why they matter in embedded programming

Beginner Tip: If you've ever set an LED or configured a timer register by setting a bit, you've already used bitwise operators — they're your toolkit for hardware-level control.

Final Thought: Bitwise operators are a core part of embedded C. Understanding them not only improves your code efficiency but also deepens your control over hardware functionality.

Interview Question 29: What Is the Use of the `volatile` Keyword in C?

Why This Question Is Asked: The `volatile` keyword is critical in embedded C to prevent compiler optimizations that could disrupt hardware behavior. This question evaluates your understanding of memory access, compiler behavior, and real-time requirements.

What the Interviewer Wants to Know:

- Do you understand what `volatile` means?
- Can you explain when and why it is used in embedded systems?
- Do you know the consequences of not using it when necessary?

How to Structure Your Answer:

1. Define what `volatile` means in C
2. Explain its purpose
3. Provide examples and use cases
4. Describe what happens without it

Sample Answer: "The `volatile` keyword in C tells the compiler that a variable's value may change at any time outside the current program flow, and it should not optimize code that accesses this variable.

In embedded systems, variables linked to hardware registers, interrupts, or shared across threads should be declared `volatile`. This ensures the compiler always reads their current value from memory, rather than caching it in a register."

Common Use Cases:

- Memory-mapped hardware registers:

```
volatile unsigned int *timer = (unsigned
int*)0x40001000;
*timer = 0x01;
```

- Flags modified in ISR:

```
volatile int interruptFlag = 0;
```

- Shared variables in multithreaded or real-time applications

What Happens Without volatile:

- The compiler may optimize by skipping reads/writes
- Leads to incorrect behavior in polling loops or interrupt checks

Example Problem Without volatile:

```
while(flag == 0); // may become an infinite loop if
compiler optimizes it
```

Correct Usage:

```
volatile int flag = 0;
while(flag == 0); // compiler always checks memory
```

Do and Don't Section

Do:

- ✅ Explain that volatile prevents compiler optimization
- ✅ Provide hardware-related examples
- ✅ Clarify why it's essential in embedded environments

Don't:

- ✗ Use `volatile` as a substitute for thread safety
- ✗ Forget to mention ISR and hardware register use cases
- ✗ Skip real-world consequences of omitting it

Beginner Tip: If your variable might change outside of your main program's logic — like from an interrupt or hardware — use `volatile` to avoid strange bugs.

Final Thought: Mastering the use of `volatile` is vital for writing safe, predictable embedded code. It bridges the gap between software behavior and real-time hardware changes.

Interview Question 30: What Is the Difference Between Macros and Functions?

Why This Question Is Asked: Understanding the difference between macros and functions helps evaluate your grasp of C language optimization, readability, and memory handling in embedded programming.

What the Interviewer Wants to Know:

- Can you distinguish between macros and functions?
- Do you understand how they are implemented and used?
- Are you aware of their advantages and drawbacks?

How to Structure Your Answer:

1. Define macros and functions
2. Explain how each works
3. Compare them in a table format
4. Provide examples and use cases

Sample Answer: "Macros are preprocessor directives that perform text substitution before compilation, while functions are reusable blocks of compiled code that execute at runtime. Macros are faster because they avoid function call overhead, but they can lead to errors if not used carefully.

Functions are safer and easier to debug, with type checking and scope management, but slightly slower due to the overhead of function calls."

Comparison Table:

Aspect	Macros	Functions
Type Checking	No	Yes
Compilation	Preprocessor substitution	Compiled and linked
Runtime Overhead	None (inline substitution)	Has function call overhead
Debugging	Hard to trace	Easier to debug
Scope	Global (no real scope)	Local (respects variable scope)
Parameter Handling	No evaluation safety	Safe and evaluated once
Example	`#define SQUARE(x) ((x)*(x))`	`int square(int x) { return x*x; }`

Macro Pitfall Example:

```
#define SQUARE(x) (x * x)
int result = SQUARE(2 + 3); // Expands to (2 + 3 * 2 +
3) = 11, not 25
```

Safer Macro:

```
#define SQUARE(x) ((x)*(x))
```

Do and Don't Section

Do:

- ✅ Use macros for constants and simple operations
- ✅ Use functions for complex logic and type safety
- ✅ Provide examples showing both tools in context

Don't:

- ✖ Use macros blindly for complex logic
- ✖ Forget about operator precedence in macros
- ✖ Confuse function pointers with macro substitution

Beginner Tip: If you need performance and simplicity, use a macro. If you need clarity and safety, use a function.

Final Thought: Both macros and functions have their place in embedded development. Understanding their differences lets you write more efficient and maintainable code tailored to your system's needs.

Interview Question 31: What Are Inline Functions?

Why This Question Is Asked: Inline functions are a key optimization feature in C/C++ programming, especially for embedded systems where performance and size matter. This question checks your understanding of how to balance performance with code maintainability.

What the Interviewer Wants to Know:

- Do you understand what inline functions are?
- Can you explain how they differ from regular functions and macros?
- Are you aware of when to use them in embedded development?

How to Structure Your Answer:

1. Define what an inline function is
2. Explain how it works
3. Compare it with macros and normal functions
4. Mention benefits and limitations

Sample Answer: "An inline function is a function defined with the `inline` keyword that suggests to the compiler to insert the function's code directly at the point of call, rather than performing a traditional function call. This eliminates the overhead of the call and return, improving performance for small, frequently used functions.

Unlike macros, inline functions support type checking, scoping, and debugging. However, the compiler may choose to ignore the `inline` request based on optimization decisions."

Syntax Example:

```
inline int square(int x) {
    return x * x;
}
```

Benefits of Inline Functions:

- Avoids function call overhead
- Type-safe and easy to debug (unlike macros)
- Maintains variable scope
- Cleaner and more maintainable than macros

When to Use:

- For small, frequently called functions
- When performance is critical and code size increase is acceptable

Comparison Table:

Feature	Inline Function	Regular Function	Macro
Compilation	Substituted at call site	Function call	Preprocessor text substitution
Type Checking	Yes	Yes	No
Debugging	Easy	Easy	Hard
Scope	Respects function scope	Respects function scope	Global substitution
Use Case	Speed without losing clarity	Code reuse, modularity	Constants, simple expressions

Do and Don't Section

Do:

- ✓ Use for small, frequently used functions
- ✓ Prefer over macros for better type safety
- ✓ Keep logic simple to encourage compiler inlining

Don't:

- ✗ Overuse with large functions (increases code size)
- ✗ Rely on the compiler always inlining (it's just a suggestion)
- ✗ Use for complex control flows

Beginner Tip: If you want the speed of macros but the safety of functions — inline functions are your friend.

Final Thought: Inline functions offer a great balance between speed and maintainability. Using them wisely can improve performance without compromising code clarity and safety.

Interview Question 32: What Are Static and Global Variables?

Why This Question Is Asked: Understanding variable scope and lifetime is essential for writing predictable, memory-efficient code in embedded systems. This question checks your grasp of variable visibility, persistence, and encapsulation.

What the Interviewer Wants to Know:

- Do you understand the difference between static and global variables?
- Can you explain their behavior in terms of scope and lifetime?
- Are you aware of their usage in embedded applications?

How to Structure Your Answer:

1. Define static and global variables
2. Explain their scope and lifetime
3. Provide usage examples
4. Compare them in a table

Sample Answer: "A global variable is declared outside of all functions and is accessible from any function within the same file or other files (if declared with `extern`). It has a program-wide scope and persists for the entire execution.

A static variable retains its value between function calls but has restricted scope. A static variable inside a function maintains its state across calls, while a static global variable is accessible only within its source file."

Example:

```
int globalCounter = 0; // Global variable

void functionA() {
    static int localCount = 0; // Static local variable
    localCount++;
    globalCounter++;
}
```

Comparison Table:

Feature	Static Variable	Global Variable
Lifetime	Entire program duration	Entire program duration
Scope	Limited to function or file	Accessible from any file (via extern)
Initializati on	One-time only	One-time only
Retains Value	Yes, between function calls	Yes
Usage	Preserve state in local functions	Share data across functions/files

Use Cases in Embedded Systems:

- **Static:** Debouncing logic, ISR state tracking, one-time configuration
- **Global:** System-wide flags, configuration settings, device states

Do and Don't Section
Do:

- ✓ Use static for encapsulation and data persistence
- ✓ Use global only when shared access is required
- ✓ Document usage clearly in large projects

Don't:

- ✗ Overuse global variables — can lead to tight coupling
- ✗ Confuse static duration with static scope
- ✗ Use global when local would suffice

Beginner Tip: Think of static as private memory that remembers past values, and global as public memory accessible by anyone in your code.

Final Thought: Choosing between static and global variables impacts maintainability, debugging, and memory usage. Understanding their behavior ensures safer and cleaner embedded system design.

Interview Question 33: What Is a Pointer?

Why This Question Is Asked: Pointers are fundamental in C programming, especially in embedded systems where direct memory access is common. This question evaluates your understanding of memory addressing, dynamic data structures, and low-level data manipulation.

What the Interviewer Wants to Know:

- Do you understand what a pointer is and how it works?
- Can you use pointers to manipulate memory and hardware?
- Are you familiar with syntax, dereferencing, and pointer operations?

How to Structure Your Answer:

1. Define what a pointer is
2. Explain how it works (address vs. value)
3. Provide syntax and example
4. Mention use cases in embedded systems

Sample Answer: "A pointer is a variable that stores the memory address of another variable. It allows indirect access to the variable's value, enabling powerful operations like dynamic memory management, array handling, and hardware register access in embedded systems."

Syntax Example:

```
int x = 10;
int *p = &x;      // p holds the address of x
printf("%d", *p); // dereference p to get the value of
x (10)
```

Pointer Operations:

- & (address-of operator): gets the address of a variable
- * (dereference operator): gets the value from the address stored in the pointer

Use Cases in Embedded Systems:

- Accessing memory-mapped I/O registers:

```
#define GPIO_PORT (*(volatile unsigned int*)0x40021000)
GPIO_PORT = 0x01;
```

- Handling arrays and buffers
- Passing large structures to functions efficiently

Do and Don't Section

Do:

- ✓ Use pointers for efficient memory access
- ✓ Understand and handle pointer types carefully
- ✓ Apply in memory-mapped hardware and dynamic memory tasks

Don't:

- ✗ Dereference uninitialized or NULL pointers
- ✗ Ignore pointer arithmetic side effects
- ✗ Confuse pointer value with the value being pointed to

Beginner Tip: Think of a pointer as a signpost — it doesn't hold the actual value, but shows where to find it.

Final Thought: Pointers give you powerful control over memory and data, but require precision. Mastery of pointers is key for efficient, low-level embedded programming.

Interview Question 34: What Is a Dangling Pointer?

Why This Question Is Asked: Dangling pointers can lead to undefined behavior, crashes, or data corruption. This question checks your ability to write safe and robust embedded code.

What the Interviewer Wants to Know:

- Do you understand how dangling pointers are created?
- Can you explain the risks and how to avoid them?
- Do you practice safe pointer usage?

How to Structure Your Answer:

1. Define what a dangling pointer is
2. Explain how it is created and why it's dangerous
3. Show a simple code example
4. List best practices for prevention

Sample Answer: "A dangling pointer is a pointer that continues to reference a memory location after the object it points to has been deallocated or gone out of scope. Accessing such pointers can lead to undefined behavior."

Common Causes:

- Freeing memory and not nullifying the pointer
- Returning addresses of local variables from a function

Example:

```
int* getPointer() {
    int local = 5;
    return &local; // returning address of local
variable
}
```

Best Practices to Avoid Dangling Pointers:

- Set pointers to NULL after freeing
- Avoid returning local variable addresses
- Use static/local variables only within their scope

Do and Don't Section

Do:

- ✓ Use pointers with proper memory management
- ✓ Set to NULL after `free()`
- ✓ Validate before dereferencing

Don't:

- ✗ Dereference uninitialized or freed pointers
- ✗ Return local variable addresses from functions
- ✗ Ignore compiler warnings about unsafe pointer usage

Beginner Tip: If your pointer points to something that doesn't exist anymore — it's a dangling pointer.

Final Thought: Mastering pointers is essential for efficient embedded development, and understanding pitfalls like dangling pointers helps you write safe, reliable code.

Interview Question 35: What Is a Memory Leak?

Why This Question Is Asked: Memory management is critical in embedded systems, where resources are limited. This question checks your understanding of dynamic memory allocation and your ability to write efficient, leak-free code.

What the Interviewer Wants to Know:
- Do you understand what a memory leak is?
- Can you identify how and when it occurs?
- Do you know how to prevent it in embedded systems?

How to Structure Your Answer:

1. Define what a memory leak is
2. Explain how it happens
3. Show an example
4. List ways to detect and prevent memory leaks

Sample Answer: "A memory leak occurs when a program allocates memory using dynamic allocation functions like `malloc()` or `calloc()` but fails to release it using `free()`. As a result, the allocated memory becomes unreachable but is still reserved, leading to a gradual increase in memory usage and potentially crashing the system."

Example:

```
void createLeak() {
    int *ptr = (int*)malloc(sizeof(int) * 10);
    // forgot to free(ptr); before function exits
}
```

Why It's a Problem in Embedded Systems:

- Limited memory makes leaks critical
- Long-running applications may run out of memory
- Difficult to detect without proper tools

Prevention Tips:

- Always pair `malloc()`/`calloc()` with `free()`
- Use memory pools or static memory allocation when possible
- Monitor usage with tools like Valgrind (for desktop) or custom debug logs (for embedded)
- Set pointers to NULL after freeing

Do and Don't Section

Do:

- ✓ Check for NULL after allocation
- ✓ Use consistent memory management practices
- ✓ Test long-running functions for leakage

Don't:

- ✗ Ignore dynamically allocated memory
- ✗ Forget to free memory on all control paths
- ✗ Use dynamic memory blindly in constrained systems

Beginner Tip: If you allocate memory but lose the pointer to it without freeing — you've got a memory leak.

Final Thought: Avoiding memory leaks is crucial for system stability and performance, especially in embedded environments with tight resource limits. A good developer always accounts for memory lifecycle.

Interview Question 36: What Are Structures and Unions?

Why This Question Is Asked: Understanding data organization is vital in embedded programming. This question checks your ability to use complex data types to optimize memory and organize related variables.

What the Interviewer Wants to Know:

- Can you define and differentiate structures and unions?
- Do you understand when to use each?
- Are you aware of their memory layout and access?

How to Structure Your Answer:

1. Define structures and unions
2. Explain their differences
3. Provide syntax and usage examples
4. Mention typical use cases in embedded systems

Sample Answer: "Structures and unions are user-defined data types in C that group multiple variables under a single name. A structure allocates separate memory for each member, while a union shares the same memory for all its members.

Structures are used when all members are needed at once. Unions are used when only one member is accessed at a time, which helps save memory — important in embedded systems."

Structure Example:

```
struct SensorData {
    int temperature;
    float pressure;
};
```

Union Example:

```
union DataPacket {
    int intVal;
    float floatVal;
    char byteArray[4];
};
```

Key Differences:

Feature	Structure	Union
Memory Allocation	Separate memory for each member	Shared memory for all members
Access	All members can be accessed	Only one member at a time
Size	Sum of all members	Size of the largest member
Use Case	Complex records (e.g., configs)	Efficient data format representation

Embedded Use Cases:

- **Structure:** Grouping sensor data or device status flags
- **Union:** Data conversion (int ↔ byte array), overlaying registers

Do and Don't Section

Do:

- ✅ Use structures for related variable grouping
- ✅ Use unions when memory optimization is needed
- ✅ Be cautious about active member tracking in unions

Don't:

- ✗ Assume unions store multiple values at once
- ✗ Ignore alignment and padding issues
- ✗ Use unions for incompatible data unless necessary

Beginner Tip: Structures store all data independently, while unions save space by reusing the same memory location for all fields.

Final Thought: Structures and unions are powerful tools in embedded systems — choosing the right one based on memory needs and data access patterns is key to efficient, readable code.

Interview Question 37: What Is an enum?

Why This Question Is Asked: Enumerations (enum) improve code readability and maintainability. This question checks if you understand how to define and use symbolic constants effectively in embedded C.

What the Interviewer Wants to Know:

- Do you understand the purpose of enum?
- Can you define and use it properly?
- Are you aware of its benefits in embedded systems?

How to Structure Your Answer:

1. Define what an enum is
2. Explain how it works and how values are assigned
3. Provide a usage example
4. Mention advantages and embedded use cases

Sample Answer: "An enum (short for enumeration) is a user-defined data type in C that consists of a set of named integer constants. It improves code clarity by replacing numeric literals with meaningful names. By default, the first name is assigned the value 0, and subsequent names increment by 1 unless explicitly specified."

Example:

```
enum Direction {
    NORTH,   // 0
    EAST,    // 1
    SOUTH,   // 2
    WEST     // 3
};

enum Direction dir = NORTH;
```

Custom Values Example:

```
enum StatusCode {
    OK = 200,
    NOT_FOUND = 404,
    INTERNAL_ERROR = 500
};
```

Benefits of Using enum:

- Improves code readability
- Makes debugging easier
- Prevents usage of magic numbers
- Easier to maintain and modify

Embedded Use Cases:

- Defining device states (e.g., IDLE, RUNNING, ERROR)
- Representing command IDs or sensor types
- Improving readability in `switch-case` statements

Do and Don't Section

Do:

- ✓ Use enums to define symbolic constants
- ✓ Group related values together for clarity
- ✓ Use in switch-case for readable control logic

Don't:

- ✗ Use enums where bitwise flags are required (use macros or `#define`)
- ✗ Rely on specific enum values unless clearly defined
- ✗ Forget to document the meaning of each constant

Beginner Tip: Enums are great for replacing unclear numbers in your code. Instead of writing `if (state == 2)`, write `if (state == RUNNING)`.

Final Thought: Enums make your code more intuitive and less error-prone. They are a clean way to represent related constants, especially in embedded applications with defined states or commands.

Interview Question 38: What Is the Difference Between Call by Value and Call by Reference?

Why This Question Is Asked: Function parameter passing is a fundamental concept in C. This question helps assess your understanding of data manipulation, memory efficiency, and function behavior in embedded programming.

What the Interviewer Wants to Know:

- Do you understand how data is passed to functions?
- Can you distinguish between value and reference semantics?
- Are you aware of when to use each method effectively?

How to Structure Your Answer:

1. Define both call by value and call by reference
2. Explain how each method works internally
3. Provide code examples
4. List differences and embedded implications

Sample Answer: "In call by value, a copy of the actual value is passed to the function. Changes made inside the function do not affect the original variable.

In call by reference, the address (or pointer) of the variable is passed, allowing the function to modify the original value."

Call by Value Example:

```
void modify(int x) {
    x = x + 10; // Only modifies local copy
}
```

Call by Reference Example:

```
void modify(int *x) {
    *x = *x + 10; // Modifies original value
}
```

Comparison Table:

Feature	Call by Value	Call by Reference
Data Passed	Copy of the variable	Address of the variable
Changes Affect Caller	No	Yes
Memory Usage	More (copies data)	Less (passes address only)
Use Case	When modification is not needed	When function needs to modify data
Safety	Safer (original remains unchanged)	Riskier (original can be altered)

Use Cases in Embedded Systems:

- **Call by Value:** Constants, configuration flags, timers
- **Call by Reference:** Sensor data arrays, hardware registers, large structures

Do and Don't Section

Do:

- ✓ Use value for small, read-only parameters
- ✓ Use reference for large or modifiable data
- ✓ Document reference-based functions clearly

Don't:

- ✗ Pass large structures by value (wastes memory)
- ✗ Forget to dereference when modifying via pointer
- ✗ Modify data unintentionally when using references

Beginner Tip: Call by value makes a copy. Call by reference gives the real thing.

Final Thought: Choosing the right passing method is key to writing efficient and safe embedded code. Understanding the difference helps optimize memory use and control program behavior effectively.

Interview Question 39: What Is Recursion?

Why This Question Is Asked: Recursion is a fundamental programming concept. This question evaluates your understanding of recursive logic, stack usage, and when it's appropriate — especially in memory-constrained embedded environments.

What the Interviewer Wants to Know:

- Can you define recursion?
- Do you understand how it works behind the scenes?
- Can you identify when (and when not) to use it in embedded programming?

How to Structure Your Answer:

1. Define recursion clearly
2. Explain how it works (function calling itself)
3. Show an example (factorial, Fibonacci, etc.)
4. Mention pros, cons, and embedded considerations

Sample Answer: "Recursion is a programming technique where a function calls itself to solve a problem. Each call solves a smaller subproblem until a base condition is met. Recursive functions are elegant but can be memory-intensive due to call stack usage."

Example:

```
int factorial(int n) {
    if (n == 0) return 1;
    else return n * factorial(n - 1);
}
```

Key Concepts:

- **Base Case:** Condition to stop recursion (e.g., n == 0)
- **Recursive Case:** The function calls itself with a smaller argument
- **Call Stack:** Each recursive call consumes stack memory

Pros:

- Cleaner code for problems naturally recursive (e.g., tree traversal)
- Easier to write and understand in some cases

Cons:

- High stack memory usage
- Risk of stack overflow if base case is incorrect
- Slower in some cases due to repeated function calls

Embedded Considerations:

- Avoid deep recursion in low-memory systems
- Prefer iteration over recursion when possible
- Use tail recursion (if supported) or iterative alternatives

Do and Don't Section

Do:

- ✅ Ensure a valid base case exists
- ✅ Use for small, well-bounded problems
- ✅ Monitor stack depth in embedded systems

Don't:

- ✗ Use recursion for large or infinite cases without limits
- ✗ Forget the return values from recursive calls
- ✗ Rely on recursion in performance-critical embedded loops

Beginner Tip: Recursion is like asking a friend to help you do a task, who then asks another friend, and so on — until someone finishes it and passes the result back up the chain.

Final Thought: Recursion can simplify problem-solving but must be used with caution in embedded systems due to limited stack space. Mastering it shows depth in logic and programming control.

Interview Question 39: What Is Recursion?

Why This Question Is Asked: Recursion is a core programming concept. In embedded systems, it must be used with caution due to limited memory. This question helps assess your grasp of algorithmic thinking and memory management.

What the Interviewer Wants to Know:

- Can you define recursion clearly?
- Do you know how recursion works internally?
- Can you evaluate its pros and cons for embedded systems?

How to Structure Your Answer:

1. Define recursion
2. Describe base and recursive cases
3. Give a simple example
4. Mention memory and performance considerations

Sample Answer: "Recursion is a technique where a function calls itself to solve a smaller instance of the same problem. It continues calling itself until a base condition is met, which stops further recursion."

Example (Factorial):

```
int factorial(int n) {
    if (n == 0) return 1;          // base case
    else return n * factorial(n - 1); // recursive case
}
```

Key Concepts:

- **Base Case:** Prevents infinite recursion
- **Recursive Case:** Solves a smaller problem
- **Call Stack:** Each recursive call uses stack memory

Pros:

- Cleaner code for naturally recursive problems (trees, backtracking)
- Easier to implement for some algorithms

Cons:

- Stack overflow risk if recursion is too deep
- Performance overhead due to repeated calls
- Inefficient in memory-constrained embedded systems

When to Use in Embedded:

- For shallow recursion (e.g., nested menu navigation)
- When readability is more important than performance

When to Avoid:

- In time-critical or deep computation cases
- Where iterative solutions are more memory-efficient

Do and Don't Section

Do:

- ✓ Write a proper base case
- ✓ Limit depth in embedded environments
- ✓ Consider converting to iteration if needed

Don't:

- ✘ Forget return values from recursive calls
- ✘ Rely on recursion for critical routines
- ✘ Cause infinite recursion by skipping base case

Beginner Tip: Recursion is like stacking plates — each call adds a new plate, and you must remove them in reverse order to get back to the beginning.

Final Thought: Recursion can simplify coding complex problems but requires careful use in embedded systems. Mastering it demonstrates strong logical and memory-aware programming skills.

Interview Question 40: What Is Stack Overflow?

Why This Question Is Asked: Stack overflow is a common and critical error in low-level and embedded programming. This question evaluates your understanding of stack memory and how misuse can affect system stability.

What the Interviewer Wants to Know:

- Do you understand what causes stack overflow?
- Can you identify symptoms and consequences?
- Do you know how to prevent it in embedded systems?

How to Structure Your Answer:

1. Define what a stack overflow is
2. Explain how it occurs
3. Provide examples (e.g., deep recursion, large local arrays)
4. Mention ways to detect and prevent it

Sample Answer: "A stack overflow occurs when a program uses more stack memory than is available. This usually happens due to deep or infinite recursion, or when large local variables exhaust the limited stack space. In embedded systems, where stack size is small, this can lead to system crashes or unpredictable behavior."

Common Causes:

- Deep or infinite recursion
- Declaring large local arrays or buffers
- Unchecked function calls in loops

Example:

```
void recurse() {
    int buffer[1000];
    recurse();
}
```

Consequences in Embedded Systems:

- System crash or hang
- Overwriting other memory areas
- Unexpected behavior or resets

Prevention Tips:

- Limit recursion depth
- Use dynamic or static memory instead of large local arrays
- Monitor stack usage with compiler tools or runtime diagnostics
- Use stack overflow detection flags or guards if supported

Do and Don't Section

Do:

- ✓ Test with worst-case stack usage
- ✓ Use small, efficient local variables
- ✓ Monitor stack size and growth

Don't:

- ✗ Rely on recursion for deep processing in embedded systems
- ✗ Ignore linker warnings about stack usage
- ✗ Allocate large buffers on the stack

Beginner Tip: The stack is like a box of plates — add too many, and it overflows or collapses.

Final Thought: Stack overflows are dangerous, especially in embedded environments. Preventing them is key to writing stable, memory-safe applications.

Interview Question 41: How Are Arrays Handled in Embedded Systems?

Why This Question Is Asked: Arrays are widely used for sensor data, buffers, and configuration tables in embedded systems. This question checks your understanding of memory layout, indexing, and data handling in resource-constrained environments.

What the Interviewer Wants to Know:

- Can you declare and access arrays correctly?
- Do you understand how arrays are stored in memory?
- Are you aware of best practices in embedded usage?

How to Structure Your Answer:

1. Define what arrays are
2. Explain how they are stored and accessed
3. Show syntax and examples
4. Discuss memory and performance implications in embedded systems

Sample Answer: "An array in embedded systems is a collection of elements of the same data type stored in contiguous memory locations. Arrays allow efficient access to multiple data items using indexing. They are often used for storing sensor values, communication buffers, and lookup tables."

Example:

```
int temperatureReadings[5] = {23, 25, 24, 26, 22};
for (int i = 0; i < 5; i++) {
    printf("%d\n", temperatureReadings[i]);
}
```

Memory Layout:

- Arrays are laid out contiguously in memory
- Each element is accessed via an offset from the base address
- 1D arrays are linear, multidimensional arrays are flattened row-wise

Embedded Considerations:

- Avoid large arrays on stack; prefer static or global allocation
- Watch for out-of-bounds access (no bounds checking in C)
- Use `const` for read-only lookup tables to place in Flash memory
- Align arrays properly for hardware access (e.g., DMA)

Use Cases:

- UART or SPI communication buffers
- Sensor readings history
- PWM lookup tables

Do and Don't Section

Do:

- ✓ Declare with fixed size when possible
- ✓ Use `const` for static lookup tables
- ✓ Monitor array size to avoid overflows

Don't:

- ✗ Allocate large arrays in local functions
- ✗ Access out of bounds (undefined behavior)
- ✗ Forget about memory alignment in hardware-interfaced arrays

Beginner Tip: Think of an array like boxes in a row — each one holding a value, and you access them by their position number starting from zero.

Final Thought: Arrays are simple but powerful. Efficient and safe use of arrays is essential for robust and performant embedded applications.

Interview Question 42: What Is a Circular Buffer?

Why This Question Is Asked: Circular buffers are commonly used in embedded systems for data logging, UART communication, and buffering real-time data streams. This question tests your understanding of data structures and memory-efficient design.

What the Interviewer Wants to Know:

- Can you define a circular buffer?
- Do you know how it works and how to implement it?
- Are you aware of its benefits and use cases in embedded systems?

How to Structure Your Answer:

1. Define what a circular buffer is
2. Explain how it works (head, tail, wraparound)
3. Show a conceptual or code example
4. List advantages and embedded use cases

Sample Answer: "A circular buffer, also known as a ring buffer, is a fixed-size buffer that wraps around when the end is reached. It uses two pointers — a head for writing and a tail for reading — to manage the data. When the head reaches the end, it wraps back to the beginning, reusing the space."

Key Characteristics:

- FIFO (First-In, First-Out) structure
- Constant time complexity for insertions and deletions
- Efficient memory use with fixed size

Conceptual Illustration:

```
[ 1 ][ 2 ][ 3 ][ _ ][ _ ]
  ↑           ↑
  tail        head
```

After writing two more:

```
[ 1 ][ 2 ][ 3 ][ 4 ][ 5 ]
  ↑                 ↑
  tail              head
```

Next write wraps to beginning:

```
[ 6 ][ 2 ][ 3 ][ 4 ][ 5 ]
    ↑           ↑
    head        tail
```

Embedded Use Cases:

- UART receive/transmit buffers
- Logging sensor data in real time
- Task queues or inter-thread messaging in RTOS

Simple Example:

```c
#define SIZE 5
int buffer[SIZE];
int head = 0, tail = 0;

void write(int value) {
    buffer[head] = value;
    head = (head + 1) % SIZE;
    if (head == tail) {
        tail = (tail + 1) % SIZE; // overwrite oldest
    }
}

int read() {
```

```
    int value = buffer[tail];
    tail = (tail + 1) % SIZE;
    return value;
}
```

Do and Don't Section

Do:

- ✅ Use for consistent throughput with limited memory
- ✅ Track head and tail pointers carefully
- ✅ Use modulo operation for wrapping

Don't:

- ❌ Forget to handle overflow/overlap conditions
- ❌ Allow head to overtake tail without logic
- ❌ Use dynamic resizing (circular buffers are fixed-size)

Beginner Tip: Think of a circular buffer like seats in a round table — once you reach the last seat, you start again from the first.

Final Thought: Circular buffers are efficient and predictable — two traits that are essential in embedded systems. Knowing how to implement one demonstrates practical, memory-aware coding skills.

Interview Question 43: What Is the Size of `int`, `float`, and `char` on 8/16/32-Bit Systems?

Why This Question Is Asked: Understanding data type sizes is critical for writing portable and memory-efficient embedded code. Interviewers ask this to test your knowledge of architecture-specific behavior and memory alignment.

What the Interviewer Wants to Know:

- Do you understand that data type sizes can vary by system architecture?
- Can you explain how and why these sizes change?
- Are you aware of how this impacts memory and performance?

How to Structure Your Answer:

1. Explain that size depends on compiler and architecture
2. Provide typical sizes on 8-bit, 16-bit, and 32-bit systems
3. Give examples and mention the use of `stdint.h`
4. Discuss implications in embedded systems

Sample Answer: "The size of data types like `int`, `float`, and `char` can vary based on the target architecture (8-bit, 16-bit, 32-bit) and compiler. While `char` is almost always 1 byte, the size of `int` and `float` may differ. To ensure portability, it's best to use fixed-width types from `stdint.h`."

Typical Sizes by Architecture:

Data Type	8-bit System	16-bit System	32-bit System
char	1 byte (8 bits)	1 byte (8 bits)	1 byte (8 bits)
int	2 bytes (16 bits)	2 bytes (16 bits)	4 bytes (32 bits)
float	4 bytes (32 bits)*	4 bytes (32 bits)*	4 bytes (32 bits)

* May not be supported natively on 8-bit systems and require software emulation.

Fixed-Width Integer Types (Recommended):

- `int8_t` (8 bits)
- `int16_t` (16 bits)
- `int32_t` (32 bits)
- `uint8_t`, `uint16_t`, etc.

Embedded System Considerations:

- Avoid assumptions about size: use `sizeof()` or fixed-width types
- Watch out for padding and alignment issues in structures
- Consider performance: accessing smaller types may be faster on small architectures

Do and Don't Section

Do:

- ✓ Use `stdint.h` for portability
- ✓ Test `sizeof()` on your target platform
- ✓ Understand the memory layout implications

Don't:

- ✗ Assume `int` is always 4 bytes
- ✗ Mix data types blindly in structures
- ✗ Ignore alignment and overflow issues

Beginner Tip: If you want consistency, use types like `uint16_t` instead of just `int` — you'll know exactly how much space it takes.

Final Thought: Data type sizes matter in embedded systems, where every byte counts. Understanding architecture-specific sizes and using fixed-width types ensures robust, portable, and efficient code.

Interview Question 44: What Is an ISR?

Why This Question Is Asked: Interrupts are fundamental in embedded systems for responsive and efficient handling of events. This question checks your understanding of interrupt service routines (ISRs) and their role in real-time systems.

What the Interviewer Wants to Know:

- Do you know what an ISR is and how it works?
- Can you explain the rules and restrictions for writing ISRs?
- Are you aware of ISR use cases and best practices?

How to Structure Your Answer:

1. Define what an ISR is
2. Explain when and how it is triggered
3. Describe constraints and examples
4. Mention best practices in embedded systems

Sample Answer: "An ISR (Interrupt Service Routine) is a special function that is executed in response to an interrupt. When an interrupt occurs, the processor suspends the main program execution, saves its state, and jumps to the ISR to handle the event. After the ISR is executed, the processor resumes the interrupted task."

Common ISR Triggers:

- Timer overflows
- GPIO pin change
- Peripheral events (UART, ADC, SPI, etc.)

Example (Pseudocode):

```
ISR(TIMER1_OVF_vect) {
    // Code to handle timer overflow interrupt
    counter++;
}
```

Key Characteristics:

- Must be short and fast
- No return value (typically void)
- Should not use blocking functions (like delay())
- May need to clear interrupt flags manually

Best Practices:

- Use `volatile` for variables shared between main and ISR
- Minimize ISR execution time
- Keep ISRs simple: set flags, defer processing to main loop
- Avoid calling non-reentrant functions inside ISRs

Embedded Use Cases:

- Real-time sensor polling
- Communication handling (UART receive)
- Periodic tasks with timer interrupts

Do and Don't Section

Do:

- ✓ Keep ISR code short and efficient
- ✓ Use flags for deferred processing
- ✓ Protect shared variables with `volatile`

Don't:

- ✗ Use long processing or loops inside ISR
- ✗ Call delay or non-reentrant functions
- ✗ Forget to clear interrupt flags

Beginner Tip: Think of an ISR like a phone call — you pause your task, quickly respond, then return to what you were doing.

Final Thought: Mastering ISRs is essential for real-time embedded systems. Proper design ensures responsiveness, efficiency, and system reliability.

Interview Question 45: How Do You Write an Interrupt Service Routine (ISR) in C?

Why This Question Is Asked: Knowing how to implement ISRs in C shows your ability to handle asynchronous events and interact with hardware at a low level. This is a core skill in embedded system programming.

What the Interviewer Wants to Know:

- Do you understand the syntax and structure of an ISR?
- Can you demonstrate hardware-specific implementation?
- Are you aware of the rules and constraints when writing an ISR?

How to Structure Your Answer:

1. Briefly define what an ISR is
2. Explain how ISRs are written in C for embedded systems
3. Provide syntax for common microcontroller platforms
4. List rules and best practices

Sample Answer: "An ISR in C is a special function written to handle a specific interrupt source. It is triggered by the hardware interrupt vector and should be short and efficient. The syntax depends on the microcontroller and compiler used."

Example: AVR (Atmel/GCC):

```c
#include <avr/interrupt.h>

ISR(TIMER1_OVF_vect) {
    // Handle Timer1 overflow interrupt
    counter++;
}
```

Example: STM32 (HAL Library):

```c
void TIM2_IRQHandler(void) {
    HAL_TIM_IRQHandler(&htim2);
}

void HAL_TIM_PeriodElapsedCallback(TIM_HandleTypeDef
*htim) {
    if (htim->Instance == TIM2) {
        counter++;
    }
}
```

Rules and Best Practices:

- Use ISR() macro or correct interrupt vector function name
- Avoid delay functions or long processing
- Use volatile for shared variables
- Set/clear interrupt flags as required
- Keep ISR functions void and with no parameters

Common Mistakes to Avoid:

- Using non-reentrant functions inside ISR
- Forgetting to clear hardware interrupt flags
- Modifying global variables without proper synchronization

Do and Don't Section

Do:

- ✓ Keep ISRs short and responsive
- ✓ Use interrupts to set flags for main loop processing
- ✓ Refer to datasheet for correct ISR vector names

Don't:

- ✗ Use blocking calls like `delay()` or `printf()` inside ISR
- ✗ Forget to enable global and peripheral interrupts
- ✗ Handle complex logic directly inside ISR

Beginner Tip: Think of ISRs as alarms — keep your response quick, and delegate the heavy work to your main loop.

Final Thought: Writing effective ISRs in C involves a blend of syntax knowledge, timing awareness, and hardware understanding. A well-written ISR boosts responsiveness and system efficiency in embedded applications.

Interview Question 46: What Is the Use of `typedef`?

Why This Question Is Asked: `typedef` is widely used in embedded systems to improve code readability and portability. This question helps assess your understanding of abstraction and custom type creation.

What the Interviewer Wants to Know:

- Do you know what `typedef` does in C?
- Can you explain how and why it's used?
- Are you familiar with use cases in embedded development?

How to Structure Your Answer:

1. Define `typedef`
2. Explain its purpose and syntax
3. Give examples
4. Mention embedded-specific applications

Sample Answer: "`typedef` in C is used to create a new name (alias) for an existing data type. It improves code readability and makes complex declarations easier to manage. It is especially useful in embedded systems where hardware-specific types and register mappings benefit from abstraction."

Syntax:

```
typedef unsigned int uint;
typedef struct {
    int x;
    int y;
} Point;
```

Example Usage:

```
uint counter;
Point position = {0, 0};
```

Embedded Use Cases:

- Creating portable data types (e.g., uint8_t, int16_t)
- Defining structures for registers or hardware abstraction
- Aliasing pointer types for special memory regions or access

Do and Don't Section

Do:

- ✓ Use typedef to simplify and standardize your code
- ✓ Use with structs, unions, enums, and pointers
- ✓ Improve portability by using architecture-independent names

Don't:

- ✗ Overuse typedef for trivial types (e.g., typedef int myInt;)
- ✗ Hide pointer complexity unnecessarily
- ✗ Use confusing or misleading type names

Beginner Tip: Think of typedef like giving a nickname to a long or complex type. It makes your code cleaner and easier to understand.

Final Thought: typedef is a simple yet powerful tool for making embedded code more maintainable and portable. Mastering it reflects clean coding habits and hardware abstraction awareness.

Interview Question 47: What Are Compiler Optimizations?

Why This Question Is Asked: Compiler optimizations are crucial for improving the performance, size, and efficiency of code — especially in embedded systems. This question checks your understanding of how compilers enhance code execution without altering functionality.

What the Interviewer Wants to Know:

- Do you understand what compiler optimizations are?
- Can you name common types of optimizations?
- Are you aware of their impact in embedded programming?

How to Structure Your Answer:

1. Define compiler optimizations
2. Describe common types and techniques
3. Explain benefits and trade-offs
4. Provide embedded-specific examples

Sample Answer: "Compiler optimizations are techniques applied by the compiler to improve code performance, reduce memory usage, or decrease power consumption without changing program behavior. They are especially important in embedded systems where resources are limited."

Common Compiler Optimizations:

- **Dead Code Elimination:** Removes code that is never executed
- **Loop Unrolling:** Speeds up loops by reducing iteration overhead
- **Constant Folding:** Computes constant expressions at compile time
- **Inlining:** Replaces function calls with the actual code to eliminate

call overhead
- **Register Allocation:** Uses CPU registers efficiently instead of RAM
- **Instruction Scheduling:** Reorders instructions to minimize stalls and improve pipeline usage

Example (Before and After Constant Folding):

```
int a = 3 * 4; // compiler replaces with int a = 12;
```

Embedded Use Cases:

- Reducing binary size in microcontrollers
- Improving execution speed of time-critical functions
- Enhancing battery life in low-power applications

Trade-offs:

- Optimizations may reduce code readability in debug builds
- Aggressive optimization can lead to unexpected behavior if code relies on undefined behavior

Controlling Optimizations:

- Use flags like -O0, -O1, -O2, -O3, -Os in GCC
- Use `volatile` to prevent unwanted optimization of I/O or interrupt-related code

Do and Don't Section

Do:

- ✓ Enable appropriate optimization levels for release builds
- ✓ Test thoroughly when using high optimization
- ✓ Understand the impact of `volatile`, `inline`, and `const`

Don't:

- ✖ Assume all optimizations are safe without testing
- ✖ Debug optimized builds without understanding code transformation
- ✖ Use -O3 blindly in low-memory devices

Beginner Tip: Compiler optimizations are like a smart assistant — they help improve your code automatically, but you need to understand what they're changing.

Final Thought: Compiler optimizations make embedded software faster and leaner. Understanding how they work gives you better control over performance, memory, and reliability.

Interview Question 48: What Are Common Memory Models in Embedded Systems?

Why This Question Is Asked: Memory models define how different types of memory are accessed and managed in embedded systems. Understanding them is key to designing efficient, reliable software for resource-constrained hardware.

What the Interviewer Wants to Know:

- Are you aware of how memory is structured in embedded systems?
- Can you describe different memory types and their uses?
- Do you understand the trade-offs between memory models?

How to Structure Your Answer:

1. Define what a memory model is in embedded systems
2. List and describe common types of memory
3. Discuss typical architectures and their memory segmentation
4. Highlight trade-offs and use cases

Sample Answer: "A memory model in embedded systems describes how code, data, and stack are stored and accessed in various memory regions. This model depends on the microcontroller's architecture and compiler. Understanding memory models is essential for optimizing memory usage and ensuring correct program behavior."

Common Memory Types:

- **Code/Program Memory (Flash/ROM):** Stores firmware (non-volatile)
- **Data Memory (RAM):** Stores variables and stack (volatile)
- **EEPROM/Flash Data:** Stores non-volatile runtime data

Memory Segments in Embedded C:

- **.text:** Code segment
- **.data:** Initialized global/static variables
- **.bss:** Uninitialized global/static variables
- **.stack:** Function call stack and local variables
- **.heap:** Dynamic memory (if used)

Common Memory Models:

- **Harvard Architecture:** Separate buses for code and data memory (e.g., AVR)
- **Von Neumann Architecture:** Shared bus for code and data (e.g., ARM Cortex-M)
- **Small, Medium, Large Models (e.g., 8051):** Define pointer sizes and accessible memory ranges

Embedded Considerations:

- Limited RAM makes efficient memory use critical
- ROM is often larger and used for constants and lookup tables
- Accessing flash for runtime variables can be slow and wear-sensitive

Do and Don't Section

Do:

- ✓ Understand your microcontroller's memory map
- ✓ Use `const` to place data in flash
- ✓ Minimize use of dynamic memory (heap)

Don't:

- ✗ Mix up volatile and non-volatile data
- ✗ Overuse stack or heap without bounds
- ✗ Ignore linker script configuration

Beginner Tip: Think of embedded memory as shelves in different rooms — some are fast but small (RAM), some are slow but permanent (Flash), and some are temporary (stack).

Final Thought: Mastery of memory models allows you to build optimized, stable embedded applications. It's a critical skill for working close to the hardware and maximizing efficiency on limited-resource devices.

Interview Question 49: How Do You Avoid Memory Corruption in Embedded Systems?

Why This Question Is Asked: Memory corruption is one of the most difficult bugs to find and fix in embedded systems. This question checks your awareness of safe programming practices, memory management, and defensive coding techniques.

What the Interviewer Wants to Know:

- Do you understand the causes of memory corruption?
- Can you name preventive measures?
- Are you aware of safe coding patterns in embedded systems?

How to Structure Your Answer:

1. Define what memory corruption is
2. List common causes
3. Share strategies to prevent it
4. Give examples from embedded development

Sample Answer: "Memory corruption occurs when a program unintentionally modifies memory it shouldn't — often due to pointer errors, buffer overflows, or stack overruns. This leads to unpredictable behavior, crashes, or data loss. Preventing memory corruption is critical for stable embedded systems."

Common Causes:

- Buffer overflows
- Invalid pointer dereferencing
- Stack overflows
- Writing outside array bounds
- Use-after-free or dangling pointers
- Uninitialized pointers

Prevention Strategies:

- Use bounds checking with arrays
- Validate all pointers before use
- Initialize variables and pointers
- Avoid excessive stack usage
- Use `const`, `volatile`, and `static` correctly
- Prefer static memory over dynamic allocation in embedded systems

Best Practices in Embedded Systems:

- Use `static` for persistent data instead of heap
- Set pointers to NULL after `free()`
- Use stack size analysis tools and monitor usage

- Avoid recursion in memory-constrained devices
- Use memory-safe libraries and functions (e.g., `strncpy()` over `strcpy()`)

Example:

```
char buffer[10];
strncpy(buffer, input, sizeof(buffer) - 1);
buffer[9] = '\0'; // Ensure null-termination
```

Do and Don't Section

Do:

- ✅ Monitor memory access and stack usage
- ✅ Use static analysis tools and runtime checks
- ✅ Design with memory boundaries in mind

Don't:

- ❌ Trust unchecked input sizes
- ❌ Use unsafe string or memory functions
- ❌ Rely on dynamic memory without fail-safes

Beginner Tip: Think of memory like boxes in a shelf — if you grab or write outside the box, you may ruin something in the next shelf.

Final Thought: Avoiding memory corruption ensures your embedded system is safe, reliable, and bug-free. It's a key skill for any embedded developer aiming for professional-grade software.

Interview Question 50: What Are Segmentation Faults?

Why This Question Is Asked: Segmentation faults are a common runtime error in C and C++ that result from illegal memory access. In embedded systems, they indicate critical flaws in pointer or memory handling.

What the Interviewer Wants to Know:

- Do you understand what causes a segmentation fault?
- Can you identify typical code errors that trigger it?
- Are you aware of debugging and prevention techniques?

How to Structure Your Answer:

1. Define segmentation fault
2. List common causes in C/C++
3. Provide an example
4. Discuss how to detect and prevent them

Sample Answer: "A segmentation fault occurs when a program tries to access a memory location that it's not allowed to — such as dereferencing an invalid or NULL pointer, or writing to read-only memory. It leads to immediate termination of the program, and in embedded systems, may cause a crash or reset."

Common Causes:

- Dereferencing NULL or uninitialized pointers
- Buffer overflows
- Accessing freed memory (use-after-free)
- Writing to read-only memory
- Stack overflows (especially with recursion)

Example:

```
int *ptr = NULL;
*ptr = 5; // segmentation fault (invalid memory access)
```

Detection & Debugging Techniques:

- Use debugging tools (e.g., GDB, Valgrind on Linux)
- Enable compiler warnings (-Wall, -Wextra)
- Use static code analyzers
- Insert runtime null checks and assert statements

Embedded Context:

- Often leads to hard faults or resets
- Difficult to trace without debug hardware or logs
- Many MCUs lack MMUs, so error behavior can be silent or destructive

Do and Don't Section

Do:

- ✅ Initialize all pointers before use
- ✅ Check pointer validity before dereferencing
- ✅ Use safe memory functions and bounds checking

Don't:

- ✕ Dereference NULL or uninitialized pointers
- ✕ Ignore return values from memory allocation
- ✕ Use freed memory or cast pointers unsafely

Beginner Tip: A segmentation fault is like trying to open a door to a room you don't own — the system shuts you out to prevent damage.

Final Thought: Segmentation faults are serious indicators of poor memory management. In embedded systems, avoiding them ensures safety, stability, and proper resource handling.

Section 3: Microcontroller Peripherals & Protocols (51–75)

Interview Question 51: What Are Serial Communication Protocols?

Why This Question Is Asked: Serial communication protocols are foundational for data exchange in embedded systems. This question evaluates your understanding of how microcontrollers communicate with other devices using serial data formats.

What the Interviewer Wants to Know:

- Can you define what serial communication is?
- Do you understand common serial protocols?
- Are you familiar with their characteristics and applications?

How to Structure Your Answer:

1. Define serial communication
2. List and explain common serial protocols
3. Highlight differences and applications
4. Mention embedded relevance and pros/cons

Sample Answer: "Serial communication is a method of transmitting data one bit at a time over a communication channel. It is widely used in embedded systems due to its simplicity and low pin count. Common serial protocols include UART, SPI, and I2C, each with unique features suited for specific applications."

Common Serial Communication Protocols:

1. **UART (Universal Asynchronous Receiver/Transmitter)**
   a. Asynchronous (no clock line)
   b. Uses TX (transmit) and RX (receive)
   c. Simple point-to-point communication
   d. Example: Serial debugging, GPS modules

2. **SPI (Serial Peripheral Interface)**
   a. Synchronous (uses clock line)
   b. Full-duplex
   c. Uses MOSI, MISO, SCLK, SS/CS
   d. Fast and ideal for short-distance high-speed communication
   e. Example: SD cards, displays, ADCs
3. **I2C (Inter-Integrated Circuit)**
   a. Synchronous, half-duplex
   b. Uses SDA (data) and SCL (clock)
   c. Multi-master, multi-slave
   d. Good for connecting multiple peripherals
   e. Example: EEPROM, temperature sensors, RTC modules

Comparison Table:

Protocol	Type	Speed	Wires	Use Case
UART	Asynchronous	Medium (~115200 bps)	2	Serial terminals, GPS, modems
SPI	Synchronous	High (>10 Mbps)	4	Displays, memory, ADCs
I2C	Synchronous	Moderate (100 kbps–1 Mbps)	2	Sensor networks, RTC, EEPROM

Do and Don't Section

Do:

- ✓ Choose protocol based on speed, distance, and device count
- ✓ Understand pull-up requirements for I2C
- ✓ Use UART for basic, low-speed communication

Don't:

- ✗ Mix SPI and I2C on the same lines
- ✗ Overlook signal integrity at high SPI speeds
- ✗ Forget to match baud rates in UART

Beginner Tip: Think of serial communication like sending messages through a tube — one bit at a time. Each protocol is like a different type of tube with its own rules.

Final Thought: Mastering serial protocols is essential in embedded systems. Choosing the right one ensures efficient, reliable communication between components and peripherals.

Interview Question 52: What Is UART?

Why This Question Is Asked: UART is one of the most fundamental serial communication protocols used in embedded systems. This question tests your understanding of its functionality, structure, and practical applications.

What the Interviewer Wants to Know:

- Can you define UART and explain how it works?
- Do you understand its components and signal lines?
- Are you familiar with use cases and limitations?

How to Structure Your Answer:

1. Define UART (Universal Asynchronous Receiver/Transmitter)
2. Describe how UART communication works
3. Explain the typical UART frame format
4. Highlight embedded use cases and pros/cons

Sample Answer: "UART (Universal Asynchronous Receiver/Transmitter) is a serial communication protocol that transmits data asynchronously — without using a shared clock signal. It sends data one bit at a time using two lines: TX (transmit) and RX (receive). UART is widely used in embedded systems for console debugging, GPS modules, and wireless modules like Bluetooth."

How It Works:

- UART converts parallel data from the CPU into serial form
- Uses start bit, data bits (usually 8), optional parity bit, and stop bit(s)
- Both devices must agree on a baud rate (e.g., 9600, 115200)

UART Frame Structure:

```
Start Bit | Data Bits | Parity (optional) | Stop Bit(s)
    0     | 8 bits    | 0 or 1 bit        | 1 or 2 bits
```

Example Applications:

- Serial terminal communication
- Debug output from microcontrollers
- GPS modules (e.g., NEO-6M)
- Bluetooth modules (e.g., HC-05/HC-06)

Advantages:

- Simple and low-pin count (2 wires)
- Easy to implement
- Widely supported by microcontrollers

Limitations:

- Point-to-point communication only (no multi-device bus)
- Requires baud rate synchronization
- Limited speed compared to SPI or USB

Do and Don't Section

Do:

- ✓ Match baud rates on both devices
- ✓ Use UART for logging and debugging
- ✓ Use level shifters when interfacing 5V and 3.3V UARTs

Don't:

- ✗ Use UART for multi-device communication
- ✗ Forget to handle framing and parity errors
- ✗ Assume hardware flow control without verifying support

Beginner Tip: UART is like a walkie-talkie — both sides must agree on the speed of talking (baud rate) and take turns talking on their TX and RX lines.

Final Thought: UART is a simple yet powerful communication protocol. Understanding its structure and timing is essential for robust embedded system development.

Interview Question 53: How Is SPI Different from I2C?

Why This Question Is Asked: SPI and I2C are two of the most commonly used serial communication protocols in embedded systems. This question evaluates your understanding of their architecture, trade-offs, and appropriate use cases.

What the Interviewer Wants to Know:

- Do you understand how SPI and I2C work?
- Can you explain the technical differences between them?
- Are you aware of when to use each protocol?

How to Structure Your Answer:
1. Briefly define both SPI and I2C
2. Compare them by architecture, speed, wires, and functionality
3. List use cases and pros/cons
4. Provide a comparison table for clarity

Sample Answer: "SPI (Serial Peripheral Interface) and I2C (Inter-Integrated Circuit) are both synchronous serial communication protocols. SPI uses separate lines for sending and receiving data and is typically faster and simpler but requires more wires. I2C uses fewer wires and supports multi-device communication on the same bus but is slower and more complex in protocol."

SPI Overview:

- Full-duplex communication
- Uses four wires: MOSI, MISO, SCLK, SS
- Typically faster (up to tens of Mbps)
- Single master, multiple slaves (each needs a separate SS line)

I2C Overview:

- Half-duplex communication
- Uses two wires: SDA, SCL
- Supports multiple masters and multiple slaves
- Typically slower (100 kbps to 1 Mbps standard)
- Uses addressing scheme to communicate with devices

Comparison Table:

Feature	SPI	I2C
Data Lines	4 (MOSI, MISO, SCLK, SS)	2 (SDA, SCL)
Speed	Faster (up to 50 Mbps+)	Slower (100 kbps – 1 Mbps)
Complexity	Simple	More complex (start/stop, ACK)
Device Support	One master, multiple slaves	Multi-master, multi-slave
Addressing	No addressing (uses SS lines)	Addressing scheme (7/10-bit)
Use Case	High-speed sensors, displays	Low-speed peripherals, EEPROMs

Use Cases in Embedded Systems:

- **SPI:** SD cards, TFT displays, high-speed DACs/ADCs
- **I2C:** RTC modules, EEPROMs, environmental sensors

Do and Don't Section

Do:

- ✓ Use SPI for high-speed, low-wire-count systems
- ✓ Use I2C for multiple devices over short distances
- ✓ Match clock frequency to peripheral specs

Don't:

- ✗ Use I2C for high-throughput data streaming
- ✗ Share SPI SS lines without tri-state logic
- ✗ Overload the I2C bus with too many devices without testing

Beginner Tip: SPI is like having a dedicated private line with each friend, while I2C is like a shared party line where everyone has to take turns and identify themselves.

Final Thought: Choosing between SPI and I2C depends on speed, complexity, and the number of devices. Understanding their trade-offs ensures effective and reliable embedded system design.

Interview Question 54: What Are the Advantages and Limitations of SPI?

Why This Question Is Asked: SPI (Serial Peripheral Interface) is widely used in embedded systems, and understanding its pros and cons helps determine its suitability for a given application.

What the Interviewer Wants to Know:

- Do you understand how SPI works?
- Can you explain the benefits of using SPI in embedded systems?
- Are you aware of the drawbacks and when not to use it?

How to Structure Your Answer:

1. Briefly define SPI
2. List and explain its main advantages
3. List and explain its key limitations
4. Provide embedded system examples

Sample Answer: "SPI is a synchronous, full-duplex serial communication protocol commonly used to interface microcontrollers with high-speed peripherals like ADCs, DACs, and memory devices. While SPI offers fast data rates and simple implementation, it comes with limitations such as the need for more signal lines and lack of formal addressing."

Advantages of SPI

1. **High-Speed Communication**
   a. SPI supports high data rates (10+ Mbps)
   b. Ideal for time-sensitive applications like displays or ADCs
2. **Full-Duplex Transmission**
   a. Simultaneous sending and receiving of data
3. **Simple Protocol**
   a. No complex handshaking or addressing
   b. Easy to implement in firmware
4. **Low Latency**
   a. Immediate data transfer without start/stop conditions
5. **Widely Supported**
   a. Almost all MCUs include SPI peripherals
   b. Numerous SPI-compatible devices available

Limitations of SPI

1. **No Built-In Device Addressing**
   a. Requires a separate Chip Select (SS) line per slave device
2. **More Wiring Required**
   a. Minimum of four lines: MOSI, MISO, SCLK, SS
   b. Becomes complex with multiple slaves
3. **Short-Distance Communication**

      a.   Signal integrity issues over long wires at high speed

4. **No Acknowledgment Mechanism**
   a.   No built-in error detection or acknowledgment like I2C
5. **Master-Slave Limitation**
   a.   Typically supports only one master in standard mode

Embedded Use Cases:

- TFT/OLED displays
- SD cards
- Audio DACs
- High-speed ADCs

Do and Don't Section

Do:

- ✓ Use SPI for high-speed, short-distance communication
- ✓ Keep wire lengths short for better signal integrity
- ✓ Use SPI where low-latency, high-throughput is needed

Don't:

- ✗ Use SPI when many devices must share a single bus without extra logic
- ✗ Use it for long-distance or noisy environments without careful planning
- ✗ Ignore need for additional SS lines when scaling

Beginner Tip: Think of SPI like a direct highway with multiple exits — fast and reliable but you need a dedicated lane (SS) to reach each destination.

Final Thought: SPI is fast and efficient, making it a great fit for high-performance embedded applications. However, careful design is needed to manage its limitations in multi-device systems.

Interview Question 55: What Are CAN and LIN Protocols?

Why This Question Is Asked: CAN and LIN are standard communication protocols in automotive and industrial embedded systems. This question evaluates your understanding of networked communication between multiple microcontrollers or devices.

What the Interviewer Wants to Know:

- Can you define and differentiate CAN and LIN?
- Are you aware of their communication mechanisms and use cases?
- Do you understand their advantages and limitations?

How to Structure Your Answer:

1. Define CAN and LIN
2. Explain their working principles
3. Compare features and use cases
4. Highlight pros, cons, and application domains

Sample Answer: "CAN (Controller Area Network) and LIN (Local Interconnect Network) are communication protocols used to connect microcontrollers and sensors in automotive systems. CAN is a robust, high-speed, multi-master protocol ideal for critical data exchange, while LIN is a low-cost, single-master solution suitable for simple subsystems."

CAN (Controller Area Network)

- High-speed communication (up to 1 Mbps or more)
- Multi-master protocol
- Message-based (not address-based)
- Built-in error detection and retransmission
- Used in safety-critical and real-time systems
- Example Applications: Engine control units, airbags, braking systems

LIN (Local Interconnect Network)

- Lower speed (up to 20 kbps)
- Single-master, multiple-slave protocol
- Time-triggered communication (predictable timing)
- Low-cost implementation for non-critical systems
- Example Applications: Window lifters, mirror control, seat adjustment

Comparison Table:

Feature	CAN	LIN
Speed	Up to 1 Mbps+	Up to 20 kbps
Topology	Multi-master	Single-master
Error Handling	Robust with retransmission	Basic checksum only
Complexity	Higher	Simpler
Cost	Higher	Lower
Application Type	Safety-critical, real-time	Non-critical, body electronics

Do and Don't Section

Do:

- Use CAN for critical data and real-time communication
- Use LIN for low-speed, low-cost peripheral control
- Understand bus arbitration and timing constraints

Don't:

- Use LIN for time-sensitive control systems
- Overlook noise immunity when choosing protocol
- Ignore protocol stack and driver availability

Beginner Tip: Think of CAN like a multi-lane highway for essential vehicle systems and LIN as a bicycle lane for simpler tasks.

Final Thought: Both CAN and LIN have their place in embedded design. Choosing the right one ensures reliable, cost-effective communication in automotive and industrial applications.

Interview Question 56: What Is USB and How Is It Used in Embedded Systems?

Why This Question Is Asked: USB (Universal Serial Bus) is a standard communication interface for connecting peripherals to a host system. In embedded systems, understanding USB is vital for developing modern devices that interface with PCs or other USB-compatible hardware.

What the Interviewer Wants to Know:

- Can you define USB and its operating principle?
- Are you familiar with USB roles, speeds, and types?
- Do you understand how USB is implemented in embedded systems?

How to Structure Your Answer:

1. Define USB and explain its architecture
2. Describe the USB roles (host, device, OTG)
3. List USB types and transfer modes
4. Give embedded-specific applications and considerations

Sample Answer: "USB (Universal Serial Bus) is a standardized interface for communication between devices and a host controller, such as a computer or embedded processor. It supports plug-and-play, hot-swapping, and power delivery. In embedded systems, USB is used for data transfer, firmware updates, diagnostics, and device control."

USB Roles:

- **Host:** Initiates communication and supplies power (e.g., PC)
- **Device:** Responds to host commands (e.g., mouse, microcontroller)
- **OTG (On-The-Go):** Can act as both host and device

USB Types:

- **USB 1.1:** Low/full speed (1.5 Mbps/12 Mbps)
- **USB 2.0:** High speed (480 Mbps)
- **USB 3.x:** SuperSpeed (5–20 Gbps)
- **USB-C:** Reversible connector with high-speed data and power

USB Transfer Types:

- **Control:** Configuration and setup (e.g., device enumeration)
- **Bulk:** Large, non-time-sensitive data (e.g., file transfer)
- **Interrupt:** Small, periodic data (e.g., keyboard/mouse)
- **Isochronous:** Continuous, time-critical data (e.g., audio/video)

Embedded System Applications:

- USB CDC (Communication Device Class) for virtual COM port
- USB HID (Human Interface Device) for keyboards/mice
- USB MSC (Mass Storage Class) for external storage devices
- Firmware upgrade interfaces

Do and Don't Section

Do:

- Use USB for convenient host-device data exchange
- Implement class-compliant firmware (CDC, HID, MSC)
- Understand USB descriptors and endpoint configuration

Don't:

- Overlook the complexity of USB stack implementation
- Use USB for hard real-time data without careful timing analysis
- Forget USB power current limitations on the host

Beginner Tip: Think of USB like a universal handshake system—everything follows strict rules, but once connected, you can do a lot with just one wire set.

Final Thought: USB support expands an embedded system's compatibility and usability. Understanding USB roles, speeds, and firmware integration is key for modern embedded development.

Interview Question 57: What Is PWM?

Why This Question Is Asked: PWM (Pulse Width Modulation) is a key technique in embedded systems for controlling devices like motors, LEDs, and servos. This question tests your understanding of how PWM works and where it's used.

What the Interviewer Wants to Know:

- Can you explain what PWM is and how it works?
- Do you understand its components and timing?
- Are you familiar with real-world applications in embedded systems?

How to Structure Your Answer:

1. Define PWM and its basic concept
2. Explain the duty cycle and frequency
3. Describe how PWM is generated in microcontrollers
4. List common embedded applications

Sample Answer: "PWM, or Pulse Width Modulation, is a technique used to simulate an analog signal using digital output. It works by rapidly toggling a digital pin between high and low states at a constant frequency, varying the proportion of time it stays high within each period (duty cycle). PWM is commonly used for dimming LEDs, controlling motors, and generating audio tones."

Key Concepts:

- **Frequency:** How often the pulse cycle repeats per second
- **Duty Cycle:** Percentage of time the signal is high in one cycle
- 0% = always low, 100% = always high, 50% = equal high/low time

Example:

- A 1 kHz PWM signal with a 25% duty cycle means the output is HIGH for 0.25 ms and LOW for 0.75 ms in every 1 ms period.

Embedded Applications:

- LED brightness control
- DC motor speed regulation
- Servo motor position control
- Audio signal generation
- Voltage regulation in power supplies

Do and Don't Section

Do:

- Use hardware timers for stable PWM generation
- Match PWM frequency to the application (e.g., higher for LEDs to avoid flicker)
- Filter the output if a smoother analog-like signal is required

Don't:

- Use blocking delays for software PWM in time-sensitive applications
- Forget to configure output pin properly in the MCU
- Assume the same duty cycle suits all applications

Beginner Tip: Think of PWM like flicking a light switch on and off very fast — the longer it stays on each time, the brighter the light appears.

Final Thought: PWM is a versatile and efficient method for analog control using digital outputs. Mastering PWM setup and tuning is essential for real-time embedded control systems.

Interview Question 58: How Is PWM Used for Motor Control?

Why This Question Is Asked: PWM is one of the most efficient and commonly used techniques for controlling motors in embedded systems. This question evaluates your understanding of how PWM regulates speed, direction, and torque.

What the Interviewer Wants to Know:

- Can you explain how PWM controls motor speed?
- Do you understand the role of duty cycle and frequency?
- Are you familiar with motor driver circuits and safety considerations?

How to Structure Your Answer:

1. Briefly define PWM
2. Explain how PWM adjusts motor speed
3. Describe how it interfaces with motor drivers
4. List control scenarios and application examples

Sample Answer: "PWM is used in motor control to vary the average voltage supplied to a motor by adjusting the duty cycle of a high-frequency digital signal. By increasing the duty cycle, more power is delivered to the motor, increasing its speed. This method is efficient, as it minimizes power loss by switching rather than adjusting voltage levels continuously."

Key Concepts:

- **Duty Cycle:** Higher duty cycle = higher average voltage = higher speed
- **Frequency:** Must be high enough to avoid audible noise and torque ripple (typically >20 kHz for DC motors)

Common Configurations:

- **DC Motor + H-Bridge Driver:** PWM controls speed via duty cycle; direction via logic levels
- **Servo Motor:** PWM signal controls angle (1–2 ms pulse width)
- **BLDC Motor:** PWM controls each phase via MOSFETs or dedicated driver ICs

Example:

- A 12V motor driven with 50% duty cycle PWM effectively receives ~6V average, reducing speed

Embedded Use Cases:

- Fan speed control
- Line-following robot wheels
- Drone brushless motor control
- Electric vehicle traction systems

Do and Don't Section

Do:

- Use PWM with a proper motor driver (e.g., L298N, DRV8871)
- Choose the right frequency for noise and efficiency balance
- Monitor motor temperature and current draw

Don't:

- Connect a motor directly to a GPIO without a driver
- Use low-frequency PWM for fast or precision motors
- Ignore back-EMF or inductive kickback protection

Beginner Tip: Think of PWM like tapping the gas pedal — more taps per second (and longer presses) make the car go faster, but you're still switching between full throttle and off.

Final Thought: PWM-based motor control is efficient and precise. Knowing how to configure it with drivers and tune it for responsiveness and smooth operation is crucial for embedded motion systems.

Interview Question 59: What Is a Bus in Embedded Systems?

Why This Question Is Asked: Understanding buses is fundamental to grasping how components in embedded systems communicate. This question evaluates your knowledge of system architecture and data transfer mechanisms.

What the Interviewer Wants to Know:

- Can you define a bus and its role in embedded systems?
- Do you understand the types of buses?
- Are you familiar with how data, address, and control lines work?

How to Structure Your Answer:

1. Define what a bus is
2. Describe the three main types of buses
3. Provide examples of internal and external buses
4. Highlight bus architectures and embedded applications

Sample Answer: "A bus in embedded systems is a communication pathway that transfers data between different components such as the CPU, memory, and peripherals. It can carry data, addresses, and control signals. Buses enable resource sharing and are essential for modular and efficient system design."

Types of Buses:

- **Data Bus:** Carries the actual data being transferred
- **Address Bus:** Carries the memory address for data access
- **Control Bus:** Carries control signals (e.g., read/write enable)

Common Bus Architectures:

- **System Bus (Internal):** Connects CPU, RAM, ROM (e.g., AMBA, Harvard Bus)
- **Peripheral Bus (External):** Interfaces with external devices (e.g., SPI, I2C, USB, CAN)
- **Parallel Bus:** Transmits multiple bits at once (e.g., address/data bus)
- **Serial Bus:** Transmits one bit at a time (e.g., UART, SPI, I2C)

Embedded Use Cases:

- AMBA (Advanced Microcontroller Bus Architecture) in ARM Cortex-M systems
- I2C bus for low-speed sensors
- SPI bus for flash memory and displays

Do and Don't Section

Do:

- Understand timing, protocol, and bandwidth requirements for each bus
- Choose appropriate bus type based on speed and number of devices
- Use pull-up resistors where needed (e.g., I2C)

Don't:

- Mix incompatible bus types without level shifting or buffers
- Ignore arbitration mechanisms in shared buses
- Overload a bus with too many devices

Beginner Tip: Think of a bus like a delivery road system inside your microcontroller — different lanes (data, address, control) carry packages (information) between houses (components).

Final Thought: A bus is the backbone of data transfer in embedded systems. Understanding how buses operate and selecting the right one is essential for system efficiency, scalability, and communication reliability.

Interview Question 60: Explain the I2C Addressing Mechanism

Why This Question Is Asked: I2C (Inter-Integrated Circuit) is a popular protocol for connecting multiple devices using just two wires. This question tests your knowledge of how devices are identified and communicated with on the I2C bus.

What the Interviewer Wants to Know:

- Do you understand how I2C device addressing works?
- Can you explain 7-bit and 10-bit addressing?
- Are you aware of reserved addresses and address conflicts?

How to Structure Your Answer:

1. Define what I2C addressing is
2. Explain 7-bit vs. 10-bit addressing
3. Discuss address assignment and limitations
4. Mention reserved address ranges and how to avoid conflicts

Sample Answer: "In I2C communication, each device is assigned a unique address by which the master can identify and communicate with it. Most devices use 7-bit addresses, allowing up to 127 unique device addresses (0–127), though some support 10-bit addressing for larger systems. The master initiates communication by sending the address of the target device, followed by a read/write bit."

7-Bit Addressing (Common):
- Total possible addresses: $2^7 = 128$
- Usable addresses: ~112 (some reserved)
- Address frame: [7-bit address][R/W bit]
- Example: 0x3C for an OLED display

10-Bit Addressing (Less Common):

- Total possible addresses: 2^10 = 1024
- Two bytes used for address transmission
- Not widely supported on basic I2C hardware

Reserved Addresses:

- 0x00 – General call
- 0x78–0x7F – Reserved for future use or specific purposes
- Devices should not use these addresses for normal communication

Address Conflicts:

- Occur when two devices share the same address on one bus
- Resolved by using multiplexers or changing hardware address bits (if supported)

Embedded Use Case Examples:

- RTC modules (e.g., DS3231) use address 0x68
- EEPROM (e.g., 24LC256) may allow configurable address bits via hardware pins

Do and Don't Section

Do:

- Check datasheet for the default and configurable address bits
- Scan I2C bus with tools (e.g., i2cdetect) to check for conflicts
- Understand if your MCU supports 10-bit addressing if needed

Don't:

- Assume all devices support 10-bit addressing
- Use reserved addresses unless your protocol stack is designed for it
- Forget to set pull-up resistors on SDA and SCL lines

Beginner Tip: Think of I2C addresses like house numbers on a street — each device has a unique number, and the master is the mail carrier asking to deliver (write) or pick up (read) data.

Final Thought: Understanding I2C addressing is crucial for building reliable multi-device systems. Knowing how to assign, detect, and manage I2C addresses ensures error-free communication on the bus.

Interview Question 61: What Is RS232?

Why This Question Is Asked: RS232 is a long-standing standard in serial communication. This question helps determine your understanding of legacy and low-level communication protocols still widely used in embedded systems and industrial interfaces.

What the Interviewer Wants to Know:

- Can you define RS232 and its purpose?
- Are you familiar with its signaling characteristics and pinout?
- Do you understand where and why it's still used today?

How to Structure Your Answer:

1. Define what RS232 is and its communication style
2. Explain voltage levels, signal lines, and pinout
3. Describe baud rate and synchronization
4. Mention applications and modern usage contexts

Sample Answer: "RS232 is a standard protocol for serial communication that defines the voltage levels and signaling for point-to-point communication between devices like computers and peripherals. It uses higher voltage levels than TTL UART (±12V logic) and is typically used for long-distance or industrial serial connections."

Key Characteristics:

- **Voltage Levels:** Logic 1 = -3V to -15V, Logic 0 = +3V to +15V
- **Standard Connector:** DB9 or DB25
- **Lines Used:** TX (Transmit), RX (Receive), GND, and optional control lines (RTS, CTS, DTR, DSR)
- **Baud Rate:** Common rates include 9600, 115200 bps
- **Asynchronous Protocol:** No shared clock; start/stop bits used

Comparison with TTL UART:

- RS232 uses ±12V signaling; TTL uses 0–5V or 0–3.3V
- Level shifting required to interface RS232 with microcontrollers

Applications:

- Debugging serial interfaces
- Industrial control equipment
- POS terminals, modems
- Communication with older PCs and legacy hardware

Do and Don't Section

Do:

- Use RS232 for reliable long-distance serial communication
- Use level shifters like MAX232 when interfacing with TTL devices
- Match baud rate and settings on both devices

Don't:

- Connect RS232 directly to microcontroller UART pins
- Ignore handshaking lines in hardware flow control setups
- Use RS232 in systems requiring multi-device communication (use RS485 or I2C instead)

Beginner Tip: Think of RS232 as a walkie-talkie with a loud voice — it works well over distance but needs a translator (level shifter) to talk to modern low-voltage devices.

Final Thought: RS232 remains a reliable and simple method of communication in many embedded and industrial environments. Knowing how to work with RS232 is essential for supporting legacy systems and robust point-to-point communication.

Interview Question 62: What Is RS485 and Where Is It Used?

Why This Question Is Asked: RS485 is a robust serial communication standard used in industrial and embedded systems. This question assesses your understanding of differential signaling, multi-drop communication, and noise immunity in real-world applications.

What the Interviewer Wants to Know:

- Can you define RS485 and how it differs from RS232?
- Are you aware of its electrical and topological characteristics?
- Do you understand typical use cases and system design considerations?

How to Structure Your Answer:

1. Define RS485 and explain its signaling method
2. Compare it with RS232
3. Describe network topology and advantages
4. List key applications

Sample Answer: "RS485 is a standard for differential serial communication that supports multi-point and long-distance data transfer. Unlike RS232, which uses single-ended signaling, RS485 uses differential pairs, providing better noise immunity and allowing multiple devices on the same bus. It's widely used in industrial automation, building control, and energy systems."

Key Characteristics:

- **Differential signaling:** Uses two wires (A and B) for each signal
- **Half-duplex or full-duplex communication**
- **Max distance:** Up to 1200 meters (4000 feet)
- **Max devices:** Up to 32 nodes (or more with repeaters)
- **Connector:** Typically screw terminals or RJ45 in industrial setups

Advantages Over RS232:

- Longer communication distances
- Multiple devices on a shared bus
- High noise immunity
- Better for harsh environments

Common Applications:

- Modbus RTU protocol in PLC systems
- Remote sensors and actuators
- HVAC systems and building automation
- Smart energy meters and grid monitoring
- SCADA systems

Do and Don't Section
Do:
- Use RS485 for reliable multi-device communication over long distances
- Terminate the bus properly with resistors at both ends (typically 120 ohms)
- Use twisted-pair cable for noise rejection

Don't:
- Mix RS485 and RS232 signaling without level converters
- Leave termination resistors out in long networks
- Exceed node count without signal boosters or RS485 hubs

Beginner Tip: Think of RS485 like a party line telephone — many people can listen and talk, but they need to take turns and keep the line balanced.

Final Thought: RS485 is essential for building scalable, reliable communication networks in industrial and embedded environments. Knowing how to use it correctly ensures stable data exchange across complex systems.

Interview Question 63: How Do You Interface a Sensor with a Microcontroller?

Why This Question Is Asked: Sensor integration is fundamental in embedded systems. This question evaluates your practical knowledge of reading sensor data, handling different signal types, and applying appropriate interfacing techniques.

What the Interviewer Wants to Know:

- Can you explain the steps to connect and read from a sensor?
- Do you understand analog vs. digital sensor types?
- Are you familiar with communication protocols and signal conditioning?

How to Structure Your Answer:

1. Identify the sensor type (analog, digital, or protocol-based)
2. Explain the electrical interface (voltage levels, pins)
3. Describe how to read data (ADC, GPIO, I2C, SPI, UART)
4. Mention initialization, filtering, and software handling

Sample Answer: "To interface a sensor with a microcontroller, first identify the sensor type — whether it's analog (like LM35), digital (like DHT11), or uses a protocol (like I2C/SPI). For analog sensors, connect the output to an ADC pin and convert the signal. For digital sensors, use GPIO or the required protocol library. Signal conditioning, proper timing, and pull-up/down resistors are essential depending on the sensor."

Types of Sensor Interfaces:

- **Analog:** Sensor outputs a continuous voltage (e.g., potentiometer, LM35)
  - Use ADC of microcontroller
  - Apply low-pass filter if noisy
- **Digital:** Simple HIGH/LOW output (e.g., PIR sensor)
  - Connect to GPIO with interrupt or polling
- **I2C/SPI/UART Sensors:** Use protocol library or write driver code
  - I2C: Connect SDA/SCL with pull-up resistors
  - SPI: Use MOSI/MISO/SCLK/CS
  - UART: Use TX/RX with level matching if needed

Steps to Interface a Sensor:

1. Power the sensor (check voltage range: 3.3V or 5V)
2. Connect output pins to microcontroller (ADC, GPIO, etc.)
3. Initialize interface in firmware (e.g., configure ADC or I2C)
4. Read data and apply calibration/formulas if needed
5. Optionally, filter or debounce data in code

Example:

- Interfacing LM35 with STM32:
  - Connect VOUT to ADC pin (e.g., PA0)
  - Configure ADC to read analog voltage
  - Convert voltage to temperature using formula: Temp = Vout × 100

Do and Don't Section

Do:

- Match voltage levels between sensor and MCU
- Read the sensor datasheet carefully
- Implement proper timing and delay for digital sensors

Don't:

- Connect analog output to digital pin without ADC
- Ignore need for external pull-up/down if specified
- Use protocol sensors without initializing communication first

Beginner Tip: Think of sensors as the senses of a robot — and the microcontroller as its brain that interprets and reacts.

Final Thought: Interfacing sensors is the core of most embedded applications. Understanding sensor types, signal formats, and microcontroller capabilities ensures accurate, efficient, and reliable data acquisition.

Interview Question 64: What Is Debounce and Why Is It Needed?

Why This Question Is Asked: Mechanical switches and buttons can produce noisy signals when pressed or released. This question evaluates your understanding of hardware/software techniques to handle unreliable input events in embedded systems.

What the Interviewer Wants to Know:
- Can you explain what debouncing is?
- Do you understand why it's necessary?
- Are you familiar with hardware and software debounce methods?

How to Structure Your Answer:
1. Define what bouncing is and why it occurs
2. Explain what debouncing means
3. Describe hardware and software solutions
4. Give examples from embedded applications

Sample Answer: "Debouncing is the process of filtering out false signals caused by the physical bounce of a mechanical switch or button. When a button is pressed or released, its contacts may briefly make and break contact several times, creating multiple unwanted transitions. Debouncing ensures only one valid state change is registered."

What Causes Bouncing?

- Mechanical vibrations during switch transition
- Can cause multiple HIGH/LOW changes within milliseconds

Debouncing Techniques:

- **Software Debounce (via delay or state machine):**
    - Add a delay (e.g., 10–50 ms) after a detected edge
    - Use a counter or timer to validate steady state
- **Hardware Debounce (RC circuit or Schmitt Trigger):**
    - Use resistor-capacitor filter to smooth signal
    - Use debounced ICs like 74HC14 or dedicated switch debouncers

Example – Software Debounce (Pseudo C Code):

```c
if (buttonPressed) {
    delay(20); // debounce delay
    if (buttonStillPressed) {
        // process valid press
    }
}
```

Applications:

- Push buttons in user interfaces
- Keypads
- Limit switches in robotics
- Rotary encoders

Do and Don't Section

Do:

- Use proper debounce method based on application criticality
- Measure actual bounce duration with oscilloscope for fine-tuning
- Combine hardware and software for high-reliability systems

Don't:

- Assume all switches are clean by default
- Skip debouncing in mission-critical input systems
- Use only delays in real-time or multitasking environments

Beginner Tip: Think of debouncing like waiting for a bouncing ball to settle before deciding if it landed in a goal.

Final Thought: Debouncing is essential for accurate and reliable user input detection. Understanding both software and hardware methods allows you to build stable, noise-resistant embedded applications.

Interview Question 65: How Do You Implement Button Debouncing in Code?

Why This Question Is Asked: This question evaluates your ability to handle real-world hardware noise through software. Button debouncing is a common embedded challenge that tests your understanding of timing, state machines, and responsiveness.

What the Interviewer Wants to Know:
- Do you know how to detect and filter button bounces?
- Can you implement software debouncing in different ways?
- Do you understand trade-offs between delay-based and state machine approaches?

How to Structure Your Answer:
1. Describe why debouncing is needed
2. Explain the two main software debounce strategies
3. Provide code examples
4. Mention which method is suited for real-time systems

Sample Answer: "Button debouncing in code is typically done by introducing a small delay after detecting a button press or by implementing a state machine or timer-based filter that confirms a stable signal over a period. The goal is to avoid reacting to false multiple presses from one physical press."

Method 1 – Delay-Based Debounce (Simple):

```
#define BUTTON_PIN 2
#define DEBOUNCE_DELAY 50 // milliseconds

int lastButtonState = 0;
unsigned long lastDebounceTime = 0;

void loop() {
  int reading = digitalRead(BUTTON_PIN);

  if (reading != lastButtonState) {
    lastDebounceTime = millis();
  }

  if ((millis() - lastDebounceTime) > DEBOUNCE_DELAY) {
    if (reading == HIGH) {
      // Button press confirmed
    }
  }

  lastButtonState = reading;
}
```

Method 2 – Timer/State Machine Debounce (Better for RTOS or Non-blocking systems):

- Sample the button every X ms
- Require a consistent state across N samples before confirming
- Uses state variables and counters

Example Logic:

```
#define BUTTON_PIN 2
#define STABLE_SAMPLES 5

int debounceBuffer[STABLE_SAMPLES] = {0};
int index = 0;

bool isDebouncedPressed() {
  debounceBuffer[index] = digitalRead(BUTTON_PIN);
  index = (index + 1) % STABLE_SAMPLES;

  for (int i = 0; i < STABLE_SAMPLES; i++) {
    if (debounceBuffer[i] == LOW) return false;
  }
  return true;
}
```

Do and Don't Section

Do:

- Use delay-based for simple systems
- Use state machine for accurate, responsive debouncing
- Keep debounce code separate from business logic

Don't:

- Use long delays that block important tasks
- Poll the button too infrequently in noisy environments
- Forget to handle button release if needed

Beginner Tip: Debouncing is about making sure the button is really pressed — not just touched by a jittery contact.

Final Thought: Software debouncing makes embedded interfaces user-friendly and reliable. Choosing the right debounce strategy helps maintain responsiveness while filtering out noise in button inputs.

Interview Question 66: What Are Analog Sensors?

Why This Question Is Asked: Analog sensors are essential in embedded systems for measuring real-world continuous signals. This question checks your understanding of how such sensors work and how their outputs are processed.

What the Interviewer Wants to Know:

- Can you define what analog sensors are?
- Do you understand how their output is read?
- Are you familiar with examples and interfacing techniques?

How to Structure Your Answer:

1. Define analog sensors and how they differ from digital
2. Explain how analog signals are interpreted
3. List common examples of analog sensors
4. Describe interfacing with microcontrollers

Sample Answer: "Analog sensors output a continuous voltage signal proportional to a physical quantity such as temperature, light, or pressure. Unlike digital sensors that output discrete values (HIGH/LOW or digital data), analog sensors provide variable voltages that must be read using an ADC (Analog-to-Digital Converter)."

Key Characteristics:

- Output is a continuous voltage (e.g., 0–5V or 0–3.3V)
- Requires analog input pin and ADC on the microcontroller
- Resolution of ADC determines sensor reading precision

Examples of Analog Sensors:

- LM35 (temperature sensor)
- LDR (light-dependent resistor)
- MQ-series gas sensors
- Potentiometers
- Force-sensitive resistors (FSR)

How to Interface Analog Sensors:

1. Power the sensor (check voltage level requirements)
2. Connect signal output to ADC pin
3. Initialize ADC in firmware
4. Convert ADC value to physical quantity using calibration/formula

Example (LM35 with STM32):

- LM35 outputs 10 mV per °C
- Read analog value via ADC
- Convert to temperature: `Temp = (ADC_Value / ADC_Resolution) * Vref / 10mV`

Do and Don't Section

Do:

- Use analog sensors for real-world continuous measurements
- Calibrate sensors for accuracy
- Filter noisy signals if necessary (hardware or software)

Don't:

- Connect analog sensors to digital-only GPIOs
- Skip ADC configuration and expect correct results
- Ignore power supply noise or grounding issues

Beginner Tip: Think of analog sensors like a dimmer switch — they don't just say ON or OFF; they tell you exactly how much.

Final Thought: Analog sensors play a vital role in capturing physical phenomena in embedded systems. Proper understanding and handling ensure accurate and responsive data acquisition.

Interview Question 67: What Are Digital Sensors?

Why This Question Is Asked: Digital sensors are widely used in embedded systems for their accuracy and ease of interfacing. This question tests your understanding of how they work and how to integrate them with microcontrollers.

What the Interviewer Wants to Know:

- Can you define what digital sensors are?
- Do you understand how their output differs from analog sensors?
- Are you familiar with their communication methods and applications?

How to Structure Your Answer:

1. Define digital sensors and how they work
2. Explain how digital signals are interpreted
3. List common examples of digital sensors
4. Describe interfacing with microcontrollers

Sample Answer: "Digital sensors provide output in discrete levels, typically in the form of binary values (HIGH/LOW) or as serial data via communication protocols like I2C, SPI, or UART. They often include built-in processing circuitry to convert analog signals internally, making them easier to use and more immune to noise."

Key Characteristics:

- Output is digital: either logic HIGH/LOW or data stream
- Often include internal ADC and signal processing
- Typically easier to interface and less prone to noise

Types of Digital Sensor Outputs:

- **Binary (On/Off):** Simple HIGH/LOW (e.g., PIR sensor, limit switch)
- **Serial Data (I2C/SPI/UART):** Structured communication (e.g., DHT11, BMP280, MPU6050)

Examples of Digital Sensors:

- DHT11/DHT22 (temperature & humidity)
- DS18B20 (1-wire temperature sensor)
- MPU6050 (accelerometer and gyroscope)
- HC-SR04 (ultrasonic distance sensor)
- TCS34725 (color sensor)

How to Interface Digital Sensors:

1. Connect power (typically 3.3V or 5V) and ground
2. Connect data or clock lines (based on protocol)
3. Use or write a library/driver to read and parse the data
4. Handle timing and protocol-specific requirements

Do and Don't Section

Do:

- Use digital sensors when high accuracy or pre-processing is needed
- Read documentation to understand the communication protocol
- Ensure proper pull-up resistors for I2C if required

Don't:

- Assume all sensors use the same logic level (check voltage compatibility)
- Mix protocols on shared lines without conflict handling
- Skip initialization steps specific to digital sensor setup

Beginner Tip: Digital sensors are like tiny smart devices — they do the measuring and talking; your job is to listen correctly.

Final Thought: Digital sensors simplify integration and improve reliability in embedded systems. Mastering their communication and setup is key to effective sensor-based design.

Interview Question 68: What Is EEPROM?

Why This Question Is Asked: EEPROM is essential in embedded systems for non-volatile data storage. This question assesses your understanding of memory types, data retention, and embedded data logging or configuration storage.

What the Interviewer Wants to Know:

- Can you define EEPROM and its key characteristics?
- Do you understand how it's used in embedded systems?
- Are you aware of its limitations and lifecycle?

How to Structure Your Answer:

1. Define EEPROM and how it works
2. Explain how it differs from RAM and Flash
3. List common uses and limitations
4. Provide interfacing examples

Sample Answer: "EEPROM (Electrically Erasable Programmable Read-Only Memory) is a type of non-volatile memory that retains data even after power is removed. It allows byte-level read/write operations and is commonly used in embedded systems to store settings, calibration data, and logs."

Key Characteristics:

- Non-volatile: retains data without power
- Electrically erasable and programmable
- Supports byte-wise read/write
- Slower write speed compared to RAM
- Limited write cycles (typically 100,000–1,000,000)

EEPROM vs. Other Memory Types:

Feature	EEPROM	Flash	RAM
Volatility	Non-volatile	Non-volatile	Volatile
Erase Granularity	Byte	Block/page	Byte
Write Cycles	~1M	~10k–100k	Unlimited
Speed	Slower	Faster	Fastest

Applications in Embedded Systems:

- Storing user configuration or device settings
- Calibration data
- Error/event logs
- Persistent counters (e.g., usage hours)

Example – Using EEPROM in Arduino:

```
#include <EEPROM.h>

void setup() {
  EEPROM.write(0, 42); // Store value 42 at address 0
  int value = EEPROM.read(0); // Read back value
}
```

Do and Don't Section

Do:

- Use EEPROM for small, infrequently changed data
- Implement wear leveling if writing frequently
- Read/write data with proper delay to ensure stability

Don't:

- Use EEPROM for fast, frequent logging
- Exceed write cycle limits unnecessarily
- Confuse EEPROM with Flash or RAM purposes

Beginner Tip: EEPROM is like a tiny notepad inside your microcontroller that keeps your notes even after a restart — but it wears out if you write too much.

Final Thought: EEPROM is a powerful tool for persistent storage in embedded systems. Knowing when and how to use it ensures data reliability and hardware longevity.

Interview Question 69: How Do You Write Data to EEPROM?

Why This Question Is Asked: Writing to EEPROM is common in embedded systems to preserve data across power cycles. This question tests your practical knowledge of memory handling, data retention, and write cycle management.

What the Interviewer Wants to Know:

- Can you explain how to write data to EEPROM?
- Are you aware of timing, size, and wear limitations?
- Do you know how to handle different microcontrollers or external EEPROMs?

How to Structure Your Answer:

1. Describe EEPROM write operation basics
2. Show an example (internal and external EEPROM)
3. Explain precautions like wear leveling and delays
4. Mention data structuring and verification methods

Sample Answer: "To write data to EEPROM, you select the memory address and write a value to it, usually using built-in functions or communication protocols. For internal EEPROM, the process is straightforward. For external EEPROMs, communication is typically done via I2C or SPI. You should consider write delays and avoid frequent writes to extend memory life."

Internal EEPROM Example – Arduino:

```
#include <EEPROM.h>

void setup() {
  EEPROM.write(0, 123); // Write 123 to address 0
}
```

External EEPROM Example – I2C (e.g., 24LC256):

```
Wire.begin();
Wire.beginTransmission(0x50); // EEPROM I2C address
Wire.write(0x00); // High byte of memory address
Wire.write(0x10); // Low byte of memory address
Wire.write(0x42); // Data byte to write
Wire.endTransmission();
delay(5); // Wait for EEPROM to complete write
```

Precautions and Best Practices:

- **Delay after write:** EEPROM needs time (e.g., 5ms) to complete the write
- **Avoid frequent writes:** Limited write endurance (~1M cycles)
- **Check if value has changed:** Only write if new data differs
- **Verify data:** Read back and compare after writing

Tips for Advanced Use:

- Store structured data (e.g., structs) by breaking into bytes
- Use wear-leveling algorithms to distribute writes evenly
- Store checksums or CRCs for integrity validation

Do and Don't Section

Do:

- Delay between writes as per EEPROM specs
- Use EEPROM sparingly for static configuration data
- Use EEPROM.update() on platforms like Arduino to reduce wear

Don't:

- Use EEPROM for high-frequency data logging
- Write the same data repeatedly without checking
- Exceed memory bounds or skip address handling in external chips

Beginner Tip: Think of EEPROM like a permanent sticky note — write on it carefully and only when needed, or the paper wears out.

Final Thought: Writing to EEPROM is simple but requires care. Understanding the limitations and optimizing your write logic ensures long-lasting and reliable data storage in embedded systems.

Interview Question 70: What Is DMA?

Why This Question Is Asked: Direct Memory Access (DMA) is an advanced embedded systems feature that boosts performance by offloading memory transfer tasks. This question evaluates your understanding of hardware efficiency and non-blocking data transfer mechanisms.

What the Interviewer Wants to Know:

- Can you define DMA and how it works?
- Do you understand when and why to use it?
- Are you familiar with DMA setup and application examples?

How to Structure Your Answer:

1. Define what DMA is
2. Explain how it operates independently of the CPU
3. Describe typical use cases
4. List advantages and implementation considerations

Sample Answer: "DMA (Direct Memory Access) is a feature that allows peripherals or memory blocks to transfer data directly to and from RAM without involving the CPU. This offloads repetitive data movement tasks from the processor, improving system performance and enabling efficient real-time data processing."

Key Characteristics:

- Bypasses CPU for memory-to-memory or peripheral-to-memory transfers
- Controlled by a DMA controller (built into most modern MCUs)
- Configurable channels and priorities
- Reduces CPU workload and latency

Common Use Cases:

- ADC or DAC continuous data streaming
- UART/SPI/I2C reception with large data buffers
- Audio/video data transfer
- Memory-to-memory copying in large arrays

DMA in STM32 Example (Pseudocode):

```
HAL_ADC_Start_DMA(&hadc1, (uint32_t*)adc_buffer,
buffer_size);
```

Advantages:

- Efficient, high-speed data transfer
- Frees CPU to handle other tasks
- Ideal for real-time and low-power systems

Challenges:

- More complex setup than CPU polling or interrupt
- Requires understanding of buffer sizes and timing
- Risk of data corruption if not synchronized properly

Do and Don't Section

Do:

- Use DMA for repetitive, high-volume data movement
- Enable DMA interrupts or callbacks for post-transfer events
- Carefully configure source, destination, and transfer size

Don't:

- Overlook synchronization between CPU and DMA
- Assume DMA is always faster for small or simple transfers
- Forget to check if peripheral supports DMA mode

Beginner Tip: Think of DMA like a helper robot — while the CPU is doing its job, DMA can handle the heavy lifting in the background.

Final Thought: DMA dramatically improves performance and efficiency in embedded systems. Mastering DMA configuration is key to building responsive, real-time applications.

Interview Question 71: What Are the Advantages of DMA?

Why This Question Is Asked: DMA (Direct Memory Access) is a key feature for optimizing performance in embedded systems. This question evaluates your understanding of how DMA benefits system efficiency, particularly in real-time and high-throughput applications.

What the Interviewer Wants to Know:

- Do you understand how DMA works in context?
- Can you clearly describe its advantages?
- Are you aware of where DMA adds the most value in embedded design?

How to Structure Your Answer:

1. List key advantages of using DMA
2. Explain each benefit in the context of embedded systems
3. Support with examples of where DMA improves performance

Sample Answer: "DMA provides numerous benefits in embedded systems, including freeing up CPU resources, enabling high-speed data transfer, and reducing power consumption. It's especially valuable in systems that handle continuous data streams or require real-time performance."

Key Advantages of DMA:

1. **CPU Offloading:**
   a. DMA handles data movement, freeing the CPU for other tasks
   b. Reduces CPU cycles spent on memory copy operations
2. **High-Speed Transfers:**
   a. Allows faster data transfer between peripherals and memory or memory-to-memory
   b. Useful for large buffer handling (e.g., audio, video, or sensor arrays)
3. **Improved Real-Time Performance:**
   a. Enables non-blocking transfers that don't interrupt time-sensitive tasks
   b. Supports concurrent data processing and transfer
4. **Power Efficiency:**
   a. Reduces CPU activity, enabling low-power modes during transfers
   b. Beneficial in battery-powered or energy-critical devices
5. **Reduced Interrupt Overhead:**
   a. Minimizes frequent interrupts by consolidating transfers into a single transaction
6. **Support for Complex Applications:**
   a. Essential for streaming applications (e.g., ADC-DMA, UART-DMA, SPI-DMA)
   b. Critical in multimedia, industrial control, and wireless communication

Examples Where DMA Excels:

- Real-time data logging from sensors to memory
- Audio playback or capture from memory to DAC/ADC
- UART/SPI communication with minimal CPU intervention
- Large frame data movement in video processing

Do and Don't Section

Do:

- Use DMA in performance-critical and continuous data applications
- Combine DMA with interrupts or circular buffers for seamless operation
- Configure DMA channels and priorities carefully

Don't:

- Use DMA unnecessarily for small, infrequent transfers
- Overlook potential race conditions between CPU and DMA
- Forget to monitor transfer completion or errors

Beginner Tip: DMA is like having an assistant who moves data while your main program focuses on critical thinking — efficiency goes up!

Final Thought: DMA offers significant performance, efficiency, and scalability benefits in embedded systems. Knowing how and when to use it effectively is a hallmark of skilled embedded design.

Interview Question 72: What Is Clock Stretching in I2C?

Why This Question Is Asked: Clock stretching is a unique feature in I2C that allows slave devices to control data flow timing. This question tests your deeper understanding of the I2C protocol, especially for timing synchronization and slave-master coordination.

What the Interviewer Wants to Know:

- Can you explain what clock stretching is?
- Do you understand when and why it's used?
- Are you aware of how it affects communication and how to handle it in firmware?

How to Structure Your Answer:

1. Define what clock stretching is
2. Explain how and when it occurs in I2C
3. Describe its role in master-slave communication
4. List implementation considerations and common issues

Sample Answer: "Clock stretching in I2C is a mechanism where the slave device holds the SCL (clock line) low to delay the master from continuing communication. This gives the slave time to process data or prepare a response before the next clock cycle. It's useful when the slave is slower or needs extra time to fetch or compute data."

How It Works:

- I2C master generates the clock (SCL)
- After sending data or address, the slave may pull SCL low
- The master must wait until the slave releases SCL (goes HIGH)
- Communication resumes when the slave is ready

Typical Use Cases:

- Slower slave devices like EEPROMs or sensors (e.g., SHT31)
- Buffer-ready or data availability signaling
- Real-time sensors that need to complete internal ADC operations

Implementation Considerations:

- Not all microcontrollers or drivers support clock stretching
- May cause issues with timeouts if not properly handled
- Ensure I2C library or peripheral is configured for stretching support

Pros:

- Synchronizes data flow between master and slower slave
- Prevents data corruption by giving the slave time to prepare

Cons:

- Increases bus latency
- May not be supported in fast-mode+ or high-speed devices

Do and Don't Section

Do:

- Enable clock stretching support in I2C driver if using slower peripherals
- Monitor SCL line behavior with an oscilloscope if issues occur
- Consider alternative flow control methods if clock stretching isn't supported

Don't:

- Ignore slave timing requirements
- Assume all I2C masters support clock stretching
- Disable watchdog timers without accounting for longer slave response times

Beginner Tip: Clock stretching is like politely asking someone to wait while you catch up — the master pauses until the slave signals it's ready.

Final Thought: Clock stretching is a vital I2C feature for maintaining reliable communication with slower devices. Understanding how it works helps you build stable and responsive I2C-based systems.

Interview Question 73: What Is Bit-Banging?

Why This Question Is Asked: Bit-banging is a low-level technique used when hardware support for communication is limited or unavailable. This question evaluates your understanding of protocol emulation, timing control, and resource-constrained programming.

What the Interviewer Wants to Know:

- Can you define bit-banging and its use cases?
- Do you understand its advantages and limitations?
- Are you aware of when to use it and when not to?

How to Structure Your Answer:

1. Define bit-banging and its purpose
2. Explain how it's implemented (timing, GPIO control)
3. List supported protocols and common use cases
4. Mention drawbacks and alternatives

Sample Answer: "Bit-banging is a technique where software manually toggles GPIO pins to simulate a communication protocol like I2C, SPI, or UART. It replaces the need for dedicated hardware modules by implementing the protocol logic in firmware. Bit-banging is useful when hardware peripherals are unavailable or already in use."

How Bit-Banging Works:

- Uses software to control pin states (HIGH/LOW) with precise timing
- Implements data transmission and reception logic
- Requires precise delays to match protocol timing requirements

Supported Protocols (Examples):

- I2C (Software I2C)
- SPI (Software SPI)
- UART (Software serial)
- 1-Wire

Common Use Cases:

- Microcontrollers with limited hardware peripherals
- Simple or low-speed communication
- Prototyping or debugging with flexible pin use

Advantages:

- Full control over protocol implementation
- Can use any available GPIO pin
- Enables use of multiple identical protocol buses

Limitations:

- CPU-intensive; no multitasking during communication
- Timing-sensitive; easily affected by interrupts
- Not suitable for high-speed or real-time communication

Do and Don't Section

Do:

- Use bit-banging when hardware modules are unavailable or limited
- Test timing carefully with an oscilloscope
- Use for low-speed, non-critical communication

Don't:

- Use bit-banging for high-speed protocols in real-time systems
- Expect consistent timing if interrupts are not disabled
- Mix bit-banging with time-sensitive tasks without caution

Beginner Tip: Bit-banging is like sending Morse code with a flashlight — you control every blink, but timing must be perfect.

Final Thought: Bit-banging is a powerful fallback for protocol emulation when hardware support is unavailable. While it offers flexibility, its timing-sensitive nature makes it best suited for low-speed or prototype applications.

Interview Question 74: What Is a Crystal Oscillator?

Why This Question Is Asked: Crystal oscillators are fundamental in providing accurate timing for embedded systems. This question tests your understanding of system clocks, frequency stability, and timing-critical applications.

What the Interviewer Wants to Know:

- Can you define what a crystal oscillator is?
- Do you understand how it works and why it's used?
- Are you familiar with common use cases in embedded systems?

How to Structure Your Answer:

1. Define what a crystal oscillator is
2. Explain its operating principle (piezoelectric effect)
3. List its applications in microcontrollers and timing circuits
4. Mention advantages and important considerations

Sample Answer: "A crystal oscillator is an electronic component that uses the mechanical resonance of a quartz crystal to generate a precise frequency signal. It's commonly used in microcontrollers and clocks to maintain accurate system timing."

How It Works:

- Based on the piezoelectric property of quartz
- When voltage is applied, the crystal vibrates at a fixed frequency
- These vibrations are converted into a stable oscillating electrical signal

Applications in Embedded Systems:

- Microcontroller system clocks
- Real-Time Clocks (RTC)
- Communication protocols requiring precise baud rates (UART, USB)
- Watchdog timers

Advantages:

- High frequency accuracy and stability
- Low phase noise
- Minimal drift over time and temperature

Comparison with Other Oscillators:

- Crystal vs RC Oscillator:
    - Crystal: Accurate, stable, slower startup
    - RC: Faster startup, less accurate, affected by temperature

Example:

- STM32 microcontroller using a 8 MHz crystal for system clock
- External 32.768 kHz crystal for RTC timing

Do and Don't Section

Do:

- Choose the correct load capacitor values based on crystal specs
- Use a crystal when accuracy and stability are required
- Place the crystal close to the microcontroller pins

Don't:

- Skip grounding and proper PCB layout considerations
- Use a crystal in high-vibration environments without precautions
- Confuse crystal oscillator with resonator or RC-based clocks

Beginner Tip: A crystal oscillator is like a tuning fork for your microcontroller — it vibrates steadily to keep everything on time.

Final Thought: Crystal oscillators are essential for precise and reliable timing in embedded systems. Understanding their operation and integration ensures accuracy in timekeeping and communication tasks.

Interview Question 75: What Is the Purpose of a PLL (Phase Locked Loop)?

Why This Question Is Asked: PLL is a crucial component in frequency control and synchronization for embedded systems. This question tests your knowledge of clock generation, signal conditioning, and system timing.

What the Interviewer Wants to Know:

- Can you explain what a PLL is and how it functions?
- Do you understand its role in embedded clock systems?
- Are you familiar with common use cases and configuration?

How to Structure Your Answer:

1. Define PLL and its basic components
2. Explain how it works (frequency multiplication and phase alignment)
3. List typical use cases in embedded systems
4. Highlight advantages and configuration considerations

Sample Answer: "A PLL (Phase Locked Loop) is a control system that generates an output signal whose phase is locked to an input signal. It's commonly used in embedded systems for clock generation, frequency multiplication, and synchronization. It ensures that the system clock is stable and accurate, even if the reference clock is low-frequency or noisy."

Key Components of a PLL:

- **Phase Detector:** Compares phase of input and feedback signals
- **Low-Pass Filter:** Smooths the output of the phase detector
- **Voltage Controlled Oscillator (VCO):** Generates an adjustable frequency signal
- **Feedback Loop:** Ensures the VCO output matches the input reference

Main Purposes in Embedded Systems:

- Frequency multiplication (e.g., boost 8 MHz crystal to 72 MHz system clock)
- Synchronize clocks between peripherals or external inputs
- Clock recovery from data streams (e.g., USB, Ethernet)
- Jitter reduction and signal conditioning

Example Use Cases:

- STM32 MCU: PLL used to scale crystal clock to higher CPU frequency
- USB PHY: PLL required to recover clock from USB data
- SDR (Software-Defined Radio): Precise frequency synthesis

Advantages:

- Enables high-frequency clocks from low-frequency references
- Maintains synchronization across multiple system clocks
- Improves timing stability and precision

Do and Don't Section

Do:
- Configure PLL for desired clock domains carefully
- Use datasheet guidelines for stability and lock time
- Monitor PLL lock status before switching clock source

Don't:

- Set PLL multipliers/dividers arbitrarily
- Change PLL settings during normal operation without precautions
- Overclock beyond rated specifications

Beginner Tip: Think of a PLL like cruise control for frequency — it locks onto a reference and keeps the system running smoothly at a steady pace.

Final Thought: PLL is vital for generating and managing system clocks in modern embedded systems. Mastering its configuration and role enables robust and synchronized device operation.

Section 4: Debugging & Tools (76–90)

Interview Question 76: What Is an Oscilloscope and How Is It Used?

Why This Question Is Asked: Oscilloscopes are essential diagnostic tools in embedded systems. This question assesses your understanding of signal analysis, timing diagnostics, and debugging hardware interfaces.

What the Interviewer Wants to Know:

- Can you define what an oscilloscope is?
- Do you know how to use it to analyze signals?
- Are you familiar with its applications in embedded development?

How to Structure Your Answer:

1. Define what an oscilloscope is
2. Describe its main functions and controls
3. Explain how it is used in embedded system debugging
4. Provide example applications and measurement types

Sample Answer: "An oscilloscope is a test instrument that visually displays voltage signals over time. It allows engineers to observe waveforms, measure signal characteristics, and debug timing or logic issues. In embedded systems, oscilloscopes are commonly used to verify digital communication, monitor analog signals, and diagnose hardware failures."

Key Features of an Oscilloscope:

- **Display:** Time on horizontal axis, voltage on vertical axis
- **Probes:** Connect oscilloscope to test points
- **Trigger Control:** Stabilizes waveform display
- **Timebase & Voltage Scale:** Adjust how signals are shown
- **Measurement Tools:** Frequency, duty cycle, rise/fall time, voltage levels

How It's Used in Embedded Systems:

- Analyze UART, SPI, or I2C waveforms
- Debug PWM signals to motors or LEDs
- Verify sensor signal quality
- Detect noise, glitches, or signal dropouts
- Check timing alignment of interrupts or GPIO changes

Common Applications:

- Confirming baud rate in serial communication
- Measuring frequency and duty cycle of PWM
- Checking analog sensor outputs
- Timing analysis in real-time embedded applications

Do and Don't Section

Do:

- Use appropriate probe settings and grounding
- Adjust time/div and voltage/div for signal clarity
- Use trigger settings to stabilize repetitive signals

Don't:

- Probe high-voltage circuits without proper isolation
- Ignore probe compensation calibration
- Overlook grounding — it can introduce noise or affect measurements

Beginner Tip: Think of an oscilloscope as a camera for voltage — it lets you see how signals change over time so you can catch electrical bugs.

Final Thought: An oscilloscope is one of the most powerful tools for embedded hardware debugging. Mastering it gives deep insight into system behavior and is invaluable for developing stable, high-performance applications.

Interview Question 77: What Is a Logic Analyzer?

Why This Question Is Asked: Logic analyzers are essential tools for debugging digital signals and protocols in embedded systems. This question tests your understanding of digital signal capture and protocol-level troubleshooting.

What the Interviewer Wants to Know:

- Can you define a logic analyzer?
- Do you understand how it's different from an oscilloscope?
- Are you familiar with its use in analyzing digital communication?

How to Structure Your Answer:

1. Define what a logic analyzer is
2. Describe its working principle
3. Compare it to an oscilloscope
4. List common use cases and benefits

Sample Answer: "A logic analyzer is a test instrument that captures and displays multiple digital signals over time. It is used to analyze the timing and logic states of digital circuits and to debug communication protocols like I2C, SPI, and UART. Unlike an oscilloscope, which shows voltage over time, a logic analyzer shows logic levels and bus states."

Key Characteristics:

- Monitors multiple digital signals (usually 8–32 channels)
- Captures binary data and displays as logic high/low
- Includes protocol decoding features (e.g., I2C, SPI, CAN)
- Triggering options to capture events of interest

Logic Analyzer vs. Oscilloscope:

Feature	Logic Analyzer	Oscilloscope
Signal Type	Digital only	Analog or Digital
Channels	Many (e.g., 8–32)	Few (usually 2–4)
Precision	High timing precision	High voltage precision
Protocol Decoding	Built-in for digital buses	Limited or optional

Common Use Cases:

- Debugging UART, SPI, I2C communication
- Capturing rare glitches or signal transitions
- Timing validation between multiple GPIOs
- Synchronizing logic signals across subsystems

Do and Don't Section

Do:

- Use logic analyzers to debug digital protocols
- Configure triggers to isolate specific events
- Label and group signals for better readability

Don't:

- Use it to measure analog voltages (not supported)
- Skip grounding all probes properly
- Ignore sample rate and buffer size limitations

Beginner Tip: Think of a logic analyzer as a digital detective — it captures and decodes your system's logic conversations so you can track what's really happening.

Final Thought: A logic analyzer is a must-have tool for modern embedded development, especially when working with digital communication and multi-signal timing issues. Mastering it can greatly speed up your debugging and validation process.

Interview Question 78: What Is JTAG?

Why This Question Is Asked: JTAG is a powerful interface used for debugging, programming, and boundary scan testing in embedded systems. This question tests your understanding of low-level hardware access and development tools.

What the Interviewer Wants to Know:

- Can you explain what JTAG is and how it works?
- Are you familiar with its use in embedded development and testing?
- Do you know its components and supported operations?

How to Structure Your Answer:

1. Define JTAG and its origin
2. Describe how it functions and its main signals
3. List common uses in embedded systems
4. Highlight advantages and tools that support it

Sample Answer: "JTAG (Joint Test Action Group) is a standard (IEEE 1149.1) interface used for debugging, programming flash memory, and boundary scan testing of integrated circuits. It allows direct access to the internals of a chip via a standardized serial protocol and is essential for development and diagnostics."

Key Features of JTAG:

- Standardized 4 or 5 wire interface: TDI, TDO, TCK, TMS (and optionally TRST)
- Provides access to chip internals for debugging and testing
- Used for programming flash, RAM, and configuring FPGAs
- Enables boundary scan for hardware validation without external probing

Main Uses in Embedded Systems:

- On-chip debugging (OCD) using breakpoints, step execution, register access
- Programming flash and EEPROM in production
- Diagnosing faults with boundary scan (pin-level testing)
- Real-time inspection of processor state and memory

Common Tools:

- OpenOCD (Open On-Chip Debugger)
- Segger J-Link
- ST-Link (for STM32)
- Xilinx iMPACT or Vivado (for FPGAs)

Advantages:

- Allows debugging at the hardware level without interfering with I/O
- Reduces need for physical test points and probes
- Facilitates rapid firmware development and validation

Do and Don't Section

Do:

- Use JTAG for hardware-level debugging and real-time inspection
- Ensure JTAG interface is accessible in your PCB layout
- Match target voltage levels with the debugger

Don't:

- Confuse JTAG with UART or USB debug interfaces
- Leave JTAG lines unprotected in security-sensitive applications
- Ignore clock and timing requirements for the TCK line

Beginner Tip: JTAG is like having a backstage pass to your microcontroller — it lets you see, change, and control what's happening without disturbing the show.

Final Thought: JTAG is a cornerstone of professional embedded development and testing. Mastering its use and tools gives deep insight into system behavior, especially during hardware bring-up and debugging.

Interview Question 79: What Is SWD (Serial Wire Debug)?

Why This Question Is Asked: SWD is a modern, lightweight alternative to JTAG for debugging ARM Cortex-based microcontrollers. This question evaluates your familiarity with debug interfaces and embedded development tools.

What the Interviewer Wants to Know:

- Can you explain what SWD is and how it differs from JTAG?
- Do you understand its advantages for embedded development?
- Are you familiar with its use in debugging and programming?

How to Structure Your Answer:

1. Define SWD and its purpose
2. Explain how it works and what it replaces
3. Compare it with JTAG
4. List applications and benefits in embedded systems

Sample Answer: "SWD (Serial Wire Debug) is a two-pin debug interface used with ARM Cortex-M microcontrollers. It provides a compact alternative to the traditional JTAG interface, offering similar functionality for debugging and programming with fewer physical pins."

SWD Signal Lines:
- **SWDIO (Data line)**
- **SWCLK (Clock line)**
- Optional: **nRESET** for target reset

Comparison with JTAG:

Feature	JTAG	SWD
Pins Required	4–5	2 (plus GND)
Protocol Type	Parallel (TAP)	Serial
Debug Access	Full	Equivalent (ARM)
Target Type	General	ARM Cortex only

Applications:

- Firmware debugging and stepping
- Flash programming
- Real-time memory and register access
- Used with tools like ST-Link, J-Link, and CMSIS-DAP

Advantages:

- Fewer pins required (great for small PCBs)
- Compatible with most ARM development tools
- Supports advanced debugging (breakpoints, watchpoints, semihosting)

Limitations:

- Limited to ARM Cortex-M (not for FPGAs or non-ARM cores)
- Fewer debug lines can reduce trace/debug capabilities vs JTAG

Do and Don't Section

Do:

- Use SWD when working with ARM Cortex-M devices
- Connect GND properly for reliable signal integrity
- Ensure SWD pins are not used for other conflicting functions in firmware

Don't:

- Confuse SWD with UART or other serial interfaces
- Ignore pin protection in final production boards (for security)
- Attempt to use SWD on non-ARM or incompatible chips

Beginner Tip: Think of SWD as the minimalistic cousin of JTAG — it gives you powerful debugging with just two wires.

Final Thought: SWD is a highly efficient and widely supported debugging interface for ARM-based embedded systems. Understanding SWD helps streamline development and is crucial for efficient debugging in compact hardware designs.

Interview Question 80: How Do You Debug a Program on a Microcontroller?

Why This Question Is Asked: Debugging is a fundamental skill in embedded development. This question evaluates your practical knowledge of troubleshooting tools, techniques, and workflows used to identify and fix issues in microcontroller programs.

What the Interviewer Wants to Know:

- Do you understand how to approach embedded debugging?
- Are you familiar with tools like SWD, JTAG, and UART?
- Can you describe a structured debugging workflow?

How to Structure Your Answer:

1. Describe typical debugging tools and interfaces
2. Explain different debugging techniques
3. Outline a structured approach to debugging issues
4. Mention common challenges and how to overcome them

Sample Answer: "To debug a microcontroller program, I first use a debugger interface like SWD or JTAG connected to an IDE (e.g., STM32CubeIDE or Keil). I set breakpoints, step through code, and inspect variable values. For real-time or communication debugging, I also use serial output, logic analyzers, or oscilloscopes. A systematic approach helps isolate hardware, firmware, and timing issues."

Key Debugging Tools:

- **SWD/JTAG Debuggers:** ST-Link, J-Link, CMSIS-DAP
- **Serial Console:** UART + USB-TTL for debug messages
- **IDE Debuggers:** STM32CubeIDE, Keil, MPLAB X, Atmel Studio
- **Oscilloscopes:** Monitor analog/PWM signals
- **Logic Analyzers:** Inspect I2C, SPI, UART buses

Common Debugging Techniques:

- **Breakpoints:** Pause execution at specific code lines
- **Step Execution:** Run code line-by-line to trace logic
- **Watch Variables:** Monitor real-time variable changes
- **Peripheral Registers:** Inspect and modify hardware registers directly
- **Print Debugging:** Output variables via UART for live monitoring
- **LED Indicators:** Use GPIO toggles for visual debug cues

Structured Debugging Workflow:

1. **Replicate the issue consistently**
2. **Check power, clock, and reset sources**
3. **Use breakpoints and step-through to isolate logic errors**
4. **Inspect peripheral configuration and communication buses**
5. **Use serial logs or toggled pins for status tracking**
6. **Confirm fixes with edge cases and long runs**

Do:

- Use hardware breakpoints and step-through for complex logic
- Log critical values to UART for non-intrusive monitoring
- Validate assumptions with multimeters or scopes

Don't:

- Rely only on print statements for timing-critical bugs
- Ignore hardware errata or initialization sequences
- Make changes without version control for reproducibility

Beginner Tip: Think of debugging as detective work — you need clues (tools), a suspect list (code/hardware), and a methodical plan.

Final Thought: Debugging a microcontroller involves both software and hardware insight. Mastering various tools and maintaining a systematic approach ensures efficient resolution of issues during development and production testing.

Interview Question 81: What Are Breakpoints?

Why This Question Is Asked: Breakpoints are a core feature of interactive debugging in embedded systems. This question assesses your understanding of runtime control, program inspection, and how to use breakpoints effectively.

What the Interviewer Wants to Know:

- Can you define a breakpoint and its purpose?
- Do you know how breakpoints are used in debugging workflows?
- Are you aware of different types and best practices?

How to Structure Your Answer:

1. Define breakpoints and their function in debugging
2. Describe how they work (hardware/software)
3. List common use cases and types
4. Share tips for effective breakpoint usage

Sample Answer: "A breakpoint is a marker set in the code that causes the program execution to pause when reached. It allows developers to inspect variables, memory, and the state of peripherals in real time, making it a fundamental tool in embedded and general software debugging."

Types of Breakpoints:

- **Standard Breakpoint:** Halts execution at a specific line of code
- **Conditional Breakpoint:** Pauses only when a given condition is true
- **Hardware Breakpoint:** Used when code runs in flash or ROM (uses CPU debug hardware)
- **Watchpoint/Data Breakpoint:** Triggers when a specific variable or memory address is accessed or modified

How Breakpoints Work:

- Inserted via an IDE (e.g., STM32CubeIDE, Keil, MPLAB X)
- On reaching a breakpoint, the microcontroller halts and the debugger can inspect:
    - CPU registers
    - Stack
    - Global and local variables
    - Memory-mapped peripherals

Use Cases in Embedded Debugging:

- Debugging logic errors in conditionals or loops
- Monitoring sensor values at a specific execution point
- Verifying interrupt or event handling logic

Do and Don't Section

Do:

- Use breakpoints to trace code execution flow
- Combine with variable watches for real-time insight
- Use hardware breakpoints for flash/ROM-based debugging

Don't:

- Overuse breakpoints, which can slow down execution
- Forget to remove or disable breakpoints in release builds
- Rely solely on breakpoints for real-time issues

Beginner Tip: Breakpoints are like pause buttons in your code — they let you stop and take a look around to understand what's happening.

Final Thought: Breakpoints are essential for stepwise debugging and detailed inspection of embedded code. Knowing when and how to use different types can significantly accelerate troubleshooting and development efficiency.

Interview Question 82: What Is a Watch Window?

Why This Question Is Asked: A watch window is a powerful feature in embedded debugging environments. This question tests your understanding of real-time variable inspection and interactive program analysis.

What the Interviewer Wants to Know:

- Can you define what a watch window is?
- Do you understand how it helps with debugging?
- Are you familiar with how to use it effectively in embedded IDEs?

How to Structure Your Answer:

1. Define a watch window and its purpose
2. Describe how it works within a debugger
3. List common use cases and best practices
4. Explain how it integrates with breakpoints and stepping

Sample Answer: "A watch window is a debugging tool within an IDE that allows developers to monitor the value of selected variables in real-time as the program executes. It is useful for tracking variable changes, identifying logic errors, and observing system behavior without modifying the code."

How It Works:

- Available in most IDEs (STM32CubeIDE, MPLAB X, Keil, etc.)
- Activated while debugging (usually during breakpoint or single-step)
- Developer adds variables or expressions to the watch list
- The IDE updates the values after each breakpoint or step

Key Features:

- View local, global, and static variables
- Monitor memory addresses or custom expressions
- Highlight changed values during execution
- Evaluate arithmetic or logical expressions

Use Cases:

- Observing sensor readings in embedded firmware
- Monitoring state machines or flags in loops
- Debugging issues with stack usage or buffer overflows
- Verifying timer, counter, or PWM register values

Do and Don't Section

Do:

- Use watch windows for non-intrusive variable monitoring
- Add custom expressions for quick evaluation
- Combine with breakpoints to trace issues efficiently

Don't:

- Assume real-time updates without halting the CPU (unless live watch is supported)
- Monitor too many variables at once (can slow down IDE/debugger)
- Forget variable scope limitations (locals may be out of scope)

Beginner Tip: A watch window is like having a live scoreboard while debugging — it keeps track of what matters as you step through your code.

Final Thought: Watch windows greatly enhance visibility into embedded program execution. Using them wisely helps diagnose issues quickly and improves the overall debugging workflow.

Interview Question 83: What Is a Debug Probe?

Why This Question Is Asked: A debug probe is essential for interfacing development tools with microcontrollers. This question checks your knowledge of hardware debugging workflows and the tools used for flashing, stepping, and inspecting embedded systems.

What the Interviewer Wants to Know:

- Can you explain what a debug probe is?
- Do you understand its role in embedded development?
- Are you familiar with common types and how to use them?

How to Structure Your Answer:

1. Define what a debug probe is
2. Describe how it connects to the target MCU
3. List popular types and supported protocols
4. Explain its purpose in debugging and programming

Sample Answer: "A debug probe is a hardware interface device that connects a development computer to a target microcontroller for debugging, programming, and testing. It translates communication between the IDE and the MCU using protocols like JTAG or SWD."

Key Functions of a Debug Probe:

- Enables stepping through code, setting breakpoints, and viewing registers
- Programs flash memory on the target MCU
- Communicates over SWD, JTAG, or proprietary debug interfaces
- Allows access to memory, peripherals, and CPU state

Common Debug Probes:

- **ST-Link:** Used with STM32 devices
- **J-Link (Segger):** Versatile, widely supported probe
- **CMSIS-DAP:** Open-source ARM debug standard
- **AVR ISP mkII / Atmel-ICE:** For AVR and SAM devices

Supported Protocols:

- **SWD (Serial Wire Debug)** for ARM Cortex-M
- **JTAG** for multi-pin full access
- **ISP (In-System Programming)** for some 8-bit MCUs

Use Cases in Embedded Systems:

- Flashing firmware
- On-chip debugging (OCD) with breakpoints and variable watch
- Memory inspection and real-time register monitoring
- Production programming and hardware validation

Do and Don't Section

Do:

- Use the appropriate probe for your MCU family
- Match voltage levels between probe and target
- Keep firmware and drivers updated for compatibility

Don't:

- Swap debug interfaces (JTAG/SWD) without reconfiguring the IDE
- Forget to power the target board properly
- Connect or disconnect probes while powered without caution

Beginner Tip: Think of a debug probe as a bridge between your computer and your microcontroller — it's how you peek inside and control what's running.

Final Thought: A debug probe is a cornerstone tool for embedded development and diagnostics. Mastering its use ensures effective programming, debugging, and hardware bring-up of microcontroller-based systems.

Interview Question 84: What Is Simulation in Embedded Development?

Why This Question Is Asked: Simulation helps developers test code logic and peripheral interactions without physical hardware. This question tests your knowledge of development workflows, efficiency, and hardware abstraction.

What the Interviewer Wants to Know:

- Can you define simulation in the context of embedded systems?
- Do you understand the benefits and limitations of using simulation?
- Are you aware of simulation tools and when to use them?

How to Structure Your Answer:

1. Define simulation in embedded systems
2. Explain how it works and what it replicates
3. List tools used for simulation
4. Describe pros, cons, and when to use it

Sample Answer: "Simulation in embedded development is the process of running embedded software in a virtual environment that mimics the behavior of real hardware. It allows developers to test code logic, timing, and interactions with peripherals without needing a physical microcontroller."

Types of Simulation:

- **Instruction Set Simulation (ISS):** Emulates CPU instruction execution
- **Peripheral Simulation:** Models interactions with GPIOs, ADCs, UART, etc.
- **System-Level Simulation:** Includes full SoC with clocks, buses, memory, and devices

Popular Simulation Tools:

- **Proteus VSM:** Visual simulation of microcontrollers with virtual peripherals
- **QEMU:** Open-source emulator supporting various CPU architectures
- **Keil uVision Simulation:** Built-in ARM simulation
- **Simulink + Embedded Coder:** For algorithm-level and control system simulation

Advantages:
- No need for physical hardware during early development
- Enables rapid testing and iteration
- Helps identify logic bugs before deployment
- Useful for education and proof-of-concept projects

Limitations:

- May not fully replicate timing or electrical behavior
- Limited support for proprietary peripherals or custom boards
- Cannot test real-world sensor data or electrical noise

Use Cases:

- Early software development and debugging
- Education and training
- Virtual prototyping of embedded systems

Do and Don't Section

Do:

- Use simulation for pre-hardware software validation
- Combine with unit testing and static analysis for reliability
- Simulate hardware events (interrupts, input changes) when possible

Don't:

- Rely solely on simulation before production testing
- Ignore hardware-specific behavior or pin constraints
- Assume timing precision equals real MCU performance

Beginner Tip: Simulation is like a flight simulator for your microcontroller — it helps you practice before flying the real thing.

Final Thought: Simulation accelerates embedded software development by enabling early testing and iteration. While not a substitute for hardware testing, it's a powerful complement for building robust and efficient embedded applications.

Interview Question 85: What Is In-Circuit Debugging?

Why This Question Is Asked: In-circuit debugging (ICD) is a fundamental technique in embedded development. This question evaluates your understanding of real-time program analysis, hardware interaction, and the role of debugging tools.

What the Interviewer Wants to Know:

- Can you define in-circuit debugging?
- Do you understand how it differs from simulation?
- Are you familiar with the hardware and software setup involved?

How to Structure Your Answer:

1. Define in-circuit debugging (ICD)
2. Explain how it works with live hardware
3. Describe the tools and connections used
4. Highlight its advantages and typical applications

Sample Answer: "In-circuit debugging is the process of running and analyzing embedded software directly on the actual target hardware using a debug interface like JTAG or SWD. It allows developers to pause execution, inspect memory and registers, set breakpoints, and step through code while the program runs on the microcontroller."

Key Components:

- Target microcontroller with debug access enabled
- Debug interface (e.g., JTAG, SWD, ICE)
- Debug probe (e.g., ST-Link, J-Link, Atmel-ICE)
- IDE/debugger software (e.g., Keil, MPLAB X, STM32CubeIDE)

How It Works:

- Connect debug probe to target via SWD or JTAG
- IDE communicates with the MCU through the probe
- Developer can view variables, modify registers, and step through code in real-time

Advantages of In-Circuit Debugging:

- Works with real hardware and peripherals
- Provides real-time, accurate execution context
- Captures issues that may not appear in simulation (e.g., timing, interrupts, power)

Use Cases:

- Diagnosing bugs in running firmware
- Testing peripheral configurations
- Verifying signal transitions and I/O behavior
- Embedded hardware validation

Comparison with Simulation:

Feature	Simulation	In-Circuit Debugging
Runs on real MCU	✗	✓
Hardware access	✗	✓
Accuracy	Limited	Full (real-time behavior)
Setup complexity	Lower	Higher (requires hardware)

Do and Don't Section

Do:

- Use ICD for validating hardware-dependent code
- Set breakpoints strategically to avoid affecting real-time behavior
- Ensure proper power and signal integrity in your setup

Don't:

- Use ICD alone to replace complete testing (include simulation/unit testing)
- Overuse breakpoints in time-critical systems
- Debug sensitive systems without ensuring isolation (voltage/ground safety)

Beginner Tip: In-circuit debugging is like performing open-heart surgery — you're working on a live system while it runs, so precision matters.

Final Thought: In-circuit debugging is an essential skill for embedded developers. It provides deep insight into system behavior and enables efficient problem-solving directly on target hardware.

Interview Question 86: What Is the Difference Between Emulator and Simulator?

Why This Question Is Asked: Understanding the distinction between emulators and simulators is crucial for efficient embedded system development and testing. This question evaluates your knowledge of development tools and their appropriate use cases.

What the Interviewer Wants to Know:

- Can you explain what simulators and emulators are?
- Do you understand how they differ in purpose and implementation?
- Are you familiar with when to use each tool?

How to Structure Your Answer:

1. Define what a simulator is
2. Define what an emulator is
3. Highlight key differences in behavior, scope, and accuracy
4. Provide examples of usage in embedded development

Sample Answer: "A simulator mimics the behavior of a microcontroller or system in a software environment without executing actual machine instructions. An emulator, on the other hand, replicates the physical hardware and runs compiled code exactly as it would on the target MCU. Simulators are useful for early development and conceptual testing, while emulators provide more accurate real-time behavior and are used for detailed hardware-software debugging."

Simulator:

- Software-based representation of MCU or system behavior
- Does not execute compiled code directly
- Models logic and timing at a high level
- Example: Keil uVision simulator, Proteus VSM

Emulator:

- Hardware or firmware-based reproduction of a target system
- Executes actual binary code as on real hardware
- Can include in-circuit emulators (ICE) and QEMU with device emulation
- Example: Segger J-Link with GDB server, ARM DS emulator

Key Differences:

Feature	Simulator	Emulator
Execution Model	Interprets model logic	Executes real machine code
Accuracy	Approximate	Highly accurate
Hardware Interaction	None or very limited	Full or partial hardware-level
Speed	Fast and lightweight	Slower but precise
Cost	Usually free or low-cost	May require hardware devices

When to Use:

- **Simulator:** Early development, education, algorithm testing
- **Emulator:** Hardware-in-the-loop testing, firmware debugging, production testing

Do and Don't Section

Do:

- Use simulators for algorithm testing and quick prototyping
- Use emulators when you need hardware-level accuracy
- Switch between tools based on project phase

Don't:

- Use simulators for hardware timing validation
- Expect simulators to reflect electrical noise or real peripheral delays
- Assume emulators are always needed in early design stages

Beginner Tip: Think of simulators as sketching your idea on paper, and emulators as test-driving a prototype.

Final Thought: Both emulators and simulators are essential tools in the embedded developer's toolkit. Knowing when and how to use them helps reduce development time, improve testing accuracy, and increase overall project success.

Interview Question 87: What Are Some Popular IDEs for Embedded Development?

Why This Question Is Asked: Choosing the right development environment is key to embedded system productivity. This question tests your familiarity with commonly used IDEs and their features for programming, debugging, and managing microcontroller projects.

What the Interviewer Wants to Know:

- Can you name IDEs suitable for embedded development?
- Are you aware of the target platforms and toolchains they support?
- Do you understand the strengths and limitations of each IDE?

How to Structure Your Answer:
1. List popular IDEs for embedded development
2. Describe key features and supported MCUs
3. Mention pros and cons for each
4. Suggest when to use which IDE

Sample Answer: "Several popular IDEs are widely used for embedded development, including STM32CubeIDE, Keil uVision, MPLAB X, and PlatformIO. Each IDE supports specific microcontroller families and offers integrated tools for coding, compiling, debugging, and flashing firmware."

Popular Embedded IDEs:
1. **STM32CubeIDE** (by STMicroelectronics)
   a. Target: STM32 (ARM Cortex-M)
   b. Features: Integrated STMCubeMX, debugger, GCC-based toolchain
   c. Pros: Free, full ST support, integrated peripheral configuration
   d. Cons: Limited to STM32 ecosystem
2. **Keil uVision (MDK-ARM)**
   a. Target: ARM Cortex-M (NXP, ST, TI, etc.)
   b. Features: Professional-grade debugger, RTX RTOS integration
   c. Pros: High-performance, RTOS-aware debugging
   d. Cons: Commercial license (free version limited to 32 KB)
3. **MPLAB X IDE** (by Microchip)
   a. Target: PIC, dsPIC, AVR, SAM (ARM Cortex-M)
   b. Features: Supports MCC (code generator), simulation, in-circuit debugging
   c. Pros: Full Microchip ecosystem integration
   d. Cons: Can be slow or resource-heavy on older systems
4. **Atmel Studio**
   a. Target: AVR, SAM (ARM Cortex-M)
   b. Features: Visual Studio-style interface, simulator, debugger
   c. Pros: Great for 8-bit AVR, integrates with Atmel-ICE
   d. Cons: No longer actively updated (being replaced by MPLAB X)

5. **PlatformIO** (VSCode extension)
   a. Target: Cross-platform (ESP32, STM32, AVR, ARM, Raspberry Pi Pico)
   b. Features: Unified build system, libraries, remote development
   c. Pros: Open-source, flexible, modern workflow
   d. Cons: Steeper learning curve, requires VSCode knowledge
6. **Arduino IDE**
   a. Target: Arduino boards, ESP32, STM32 (via cores)
   b. Features: Easy-to-use interface, vast community libraries
   c. Pros: Beginner-friendly, great for prototyping
   d. Cons: Limited debugging, not suitable for complex projects

When to Use What:

- Use **STM32CubeIDE** or **Keil** for STM32 production development
- Use **MPLAB X** for Microchip PIC/AVR projects
- Use **PlatformIO** for multi-board development and modern workflows
- Use **Arduino IDE** for educational and hobby projects

Do and Don't Section

Do:

- Choose the IDE that matches your MCU and project complexity
- Leverage built-in tools like code generators and analyzers
- Consider IDE-supported debug probes and hardware compatibility

Don't:

- Use beginner IDEs for production firmware
- Overlook license costs for commercial tools
- Ignore update and community support trends

Beginner Tip: Think of an IDE like your embedded control center — it's where coding, building, flashing, and debugging all come together.

Final Thought: The right IDE streamlines development and improves productivity. Knowing the strengths of different tools helps you select the best environment for each stage of your embedded system project.

Interview Question 88: What Is the Keil IDE?

Why This Question Is Asked: Keil IDE is one of the most widely used environments for ARM Cortex-M development. This question evaluates your familiarity with professional development tools, especially in embedded C programming.

What the Interviewer Wants to Know:

- Can you describe what Keil IDE is and what it's used for?
- Do you understand its advantages in embedded projects?
- Are you familiar with its supported features and limitations?

How to Structure Your Answer:

1. Define Keil IDE and its target audience
2. Describe the key features and toolchain
3. Mention supported microcontrollers and use cases
4. Highlight pros and cons

Sample Answer: "Keil IDE, officially known as Keil MDK (Microcontroller Development Kit), is a professional integrated development environment for ARM Cortex-M microcontrollers. It provides tools for writing, compiling, debugging, and simulating embedded applications with extensive support for real-time operating systems."

Key Features:

- uVision IDE with integrated editor, project manager, and debugger
- ARMCC or ArmClang compiler toolchains
- RTX real-time operating system (RTOS) support

- CMSIS (Cortex Microcontroller Software Interface Standard) integration
- Full debugging features: breakpoints, watch windows, memory/register view

Supported Devices:

- ARM Cortex-M0/M3/M4/M7 and newer cores
- MCUs from STMicroelectronics, NXP, Silicon Labs, Infineon, TI, and more

Use Cases:

- Industrial-grade embedded firmware
- Real-time systems using RTOS
- Debugging complex embedded projects with multi-peripheral interaction

Pros:

- Highly reliable and mature environment
- RTOS-aware debugging and trace capabilities
- Strong vendor and community support

Cons:

- Commercial licensing (free version limited to 32 KB code)
- Windows-only environment (without emulation)

Comparison with Other IDEs:

Feature	Keil MDK	STM32CubeIDE	PlatformIO
Debugging Power	Excellent	Good	Moderate
RTOS Support	Built-in (RTX)	CMSIS-RTOS	Add-ons required
Licensing	Paid (limited free)	Free	Free

Do and Don't Section

Do:

- Use Keil for production-level firmware in Cortex-M projects
- Take advantage of RTOS debugging and trace utilities
- Use with ULINKpro or ULINK2 for optimal hardware debug support

Don't:

- Use Keil for unsupported MCU architectures (e.g., RISC-V, AVR)
- Expect Linux or macOS native support
- Forget to manage license keys for large-scale use

Beginner Tip: Keil is like the Swiss Army knife for ARM microcontrollers — everything from code editing to debugging is built in with precision tools.

Final Thought: Keil IDE is a premium environment designed for professional embedded developers working with ARM Cortex-M systems. Mastering Keil gives access to advanced debugging, performance tuning, and real-time embedded development capabilities.

Interview Question 89: What Is STM32CubeIDE?

Why This Question Is Asked: STM32CubeIDE is a popular all-in-one development platform for STM32 microcontrollers. This question evaluates your familiarity with vendor-provided tools, their ecosystem integration, and ease of use in embedded development.

What the Interviewer Wants to Know:

- Can you describe what STM32CubeIDE is?
- Are you aware of its features and strengths?
- Do you know how it integrates with ST's hardware and libraries?

How to Structure Your Answer:

1. Define STM32CubeIDE and its purpose
2. List its core components and supported devices
3. Explain its typical use in development workflows
4. Highlight pros and cons

Sample Answer: "STM32CubeIDE is an integrated development environment provided by STMicroelectronics for STM32 microcontrollers. It combines code editing, project management, code generation, and debugging features in one unified Eclipse-based platform."

Core Features:

- Eclipse-based IDE with GCC toolchain (Arm GCC)
- Integrated STM32CubeMX for graphical peripheral and pin configuration
- Code generation using HAL (Hardware Abstraction Layer)
- Real-time debugging and trace capabilities
- Built-in support for ST-Link debuggers

Supported Devices:

- Full range of STM32 families (STM32F0/F1/F3/F4/F7, STM32H7, STM32Lx, STM32WB, etc.)

Use Cases:

- Getting started with STM32 development
- Prototyping and production firmware development
- HAL and LL library-based project generation
- USB, RTOS, and middleware configuration

Pros:

- Free and fully featured
- Strong integration with STM32CubeMX
- Good debugging support with ST-Link
- Large community and ST documentation

Cons:

- Limited to STM32 MCUs only
- Eclipse-based UI may feel heavy or slow
- Less customizable than makefile-based systems

Comparison with Keil and PlatformIO:

Feature	STM32CubeIDE	Keil MDK	PlatformIO
Target Support	STM32 only	ARM Cortex-M	Multi-platform
License	Free	Paid (limited free)	Free
Code Generator	Built-in (CubeMX)	External (manual)	Optional
Debugger Integration	ST-Link	ULINK/J-Link	J-Link/ST-Link

Do and Don't Section

Do:

- Use CubeIDE for any STM32 project — it's fully integrated
- Leverage STM32CubeMX to simplify peripheral setup
- Use HAL or LL APIs for efficient firmware design

Don't:

- Use it for non-ST microcontrollers
- Ignore the importance of STM32Cube firmware package updates
- Overlook CubeMX code regeneration behavior when modifying user code

Beginner Tip: STM32CubeIDE is like a smart assistant that writes half of your embedded code — especially useful when configuring complex peripherals.

Final Thought: STM32CubeIDE streamlines STM32 firmware development by integrating all necessary tools in one environment. It's ideal for both beginners and professionals seeking efficient embedded system development on ST platforms.

Interview Question 90: What Is Flashing a Microcontroller?

Why This Question Is Asked: Flashing is a basic yet crucial operation in embedded development. This question checks your understanding of how firmware is written to microcontroller memory and what tools are used in the process.

What the Interviewer Wants to Know:

- Can you define what flashing means in embedded development?
- Do you know how it is done and with what tools?
- Are you aware of common pitfalls and precautions?

How to Structure Your Answer:

1. Define what flashing is
2. Explain the process step-by-step
3. Describe tools and interfaces used
4. Mention best practices and common issues

Sample Answer: "Flashing a microcontroller means writing compiled firmware into the non-volatile flash memory of the chip. This is typically done using a debugger or programmer connected through interfaces like SWD, JTAG, or UART, allowing the microcontroller to execute the desired application code after reset."

Steps Involved in Flashing:

1. Write firmware in C/C++ and compile it into a binary or HEX file
2. Connect a debug probe or programmer to the microcontroller (e.g., ST-Link, J-Link, USB-TTL)
3. Use an IDE or command-line tool to upload the firmware
4. MCU resets and runs the new code from flash

Common Tools and Interfaces:

- **Debuggers/Programmers:** ST-Link, J-Link, CMSIS-DAP, USBasp, AVR ISP
- **Flashing Software:** STM32CubeProgrammer, avrdude, OpenOCD, MPLAB IPE
- **Interfaces:** SWD, JTAG, UART, SPI, USB DFU

Best Practices:

- Verify voltage levels match between programmer and target
- Use correct firmware format (e.g., .hex, .bin, .elf)
- Enable read-back verification to ensure successful flashing
- Keep backup of production firmware versions

Common Issues:
- Wrong interface or connection
- Locked or write-protected flash regions
- Misconfigured boot pins or fuse bits
- Power supply instability during flashing

Do and Don't Section

Do:
- Check wiring and voltage before flashing
- Use verified, compiled firmware
- Monitor console logs for error messages

Don't:
- Disconnect the programmer during flashing
- Flash without knowing the effect of fuse bits or bootloader
- Overwrite calibration or protected memory regions accidentally

Beginner Tip: Flashing is like installing a new app on your microcontroller — it loads your instructions into permanent memory so the chip knows what to do after every reset.

Final Thought: Flashing is a core part of embedded workflows. Mastering it ensures smooth development, testing, and deployment of reliable microcontroller-based applications.

Section 5: Real-World Scenarios & Projects (91–101)

Interview Question 91: How Do You Reduce Power Consumption in Embedded Devices?

Why This Question Is Asked: Power efficiency is critical in battery-powered and portable embedded systems. This question assesses your understanding of power-saving techniques at both hardware and software levels.

What the Interviewer Wants to Know:

- Can you identify common strategies to reduce power consumption?
- Do you understand low-power modes and peripheral management?
- Are you aware of trade-offs and implementation challenges?

How to Structure Your Answer:

1. List general strategies for reducing power
2. Explain specific hardware and software techniques
3. Mention tools and features in MCUs that help
4. Provide practical examples

Sample Answer: "To reduce power consumption in embedded devices, I use a combination of low-power modes, clock gating, peripheral shutdown, and efficient coding practices. Selecting low-power components and optimizing sleep cycles is essential for battery-powered systems."

Hardware-Level Techniques:

- Use low-power microcontrollers (e.g., STM32L series, MSP430)
- Disable unused peripherals (e.g., ADC, UART, timers)
- Lower system clock frequency when high performance is not

needed
- Use DC/DC converters instead of linear regulators
- Optimize PCB layout to reduce leakage and EMI

Software-Level Techniques:

- Use **sleep** or **deep sleep** modes
- Schedule tasks efficiently with low-power RTOS or tickless idle
- Minimize polling; use interrupts instead
- Avoid floating GPIOs (can cause leakage)
- Optimize loops and delay functions

Power-Saving MCU Features:

- Multiple power modes: Sleep, Stop, Standby, Shutdown
- Wakeup sources: RTC, GPIO, external interrupts
- Peripheral power domains
- Clock gating and dynamic frequency scaling (DFS)

Example:

- In STM32, using `HAL_PWR_EnterSTOPMode()` to sleep the MCU and wake up with an external interrupt

Do and Don't Section

Do:

- Profile current draw using tools like the ST Power Profiler or Joulescope
- Optimize firmware to stay in active mode only when needed
- Use watchdogs and RTC for timed wakeups

Don't:

- Leave unused peripherals or GPIOs enabled
- Poll sensors unnecessarily
- Ignore leakage from improperly configured I/O pins

Beginner Tip: Think of low-power design like budgeting your energy —
only turn on what you need and sleep the rest of the time.

Final Thought: Reducing power consumption is essential for efficient
embedded systems. Combining smart hardware choices with low-power
firmware design ensures long-lasting, reliable operation especially in
energy-constrained environments.

Interview Question 92: What Is Low Power Mode?

Why This Question Is Asked: Low power modes are key to extending
battery life in embedded systems. This question assesses your knowledge
of power management techniques and microcontroller features that
reduce energy consumption.

What the Interviewer Wants to Know:

- Can you define low power mode and its role in embedded
  systems?
- Do you understand different types of low power modes?
- Are you aware of what components remain active or inactive?

How to Structure Your Answer:

1. Define low power mode
2. Explain the types of low power modes
3. Describe what gets turned off or stays active
4. Give use-case examples

Sample Answer: "Low power mode is a state in which a microcontroller
reduces or suspends internal operations to save energy. This is achieved
by slowing down or turning off the CPU, peripherals, and clocks, while
optionally allowing wake-up sources like timers or interrupts to bring the
system back to active mode."

Types of Low Power Modes (example from STM32):

- **Sleep Mode:** CPU stopped, peripherals continue running
- **Stop Mode:** CPU and most peripherals stopped, RAM and RTC retained
- **Standby Mode:** Only RTC and backup registers powered
- **Shutdown Mode:** Minimal power draw, most components turned off

What Gets Turned Off or Stays On:

Component	Sleep	Stop	Standby	Shutdown
CPU	OFF	OFF	OFF	OFF
SRAM	ON	ON	Partial	OFF
Peripherals	ON	Partial	OFF	OFF
RTC/Wakeup sources	ON	ON	ON	Optional

Common Wakeup Sources:

- Real-Time Clock (RTC)
- GPIO external interrupt
- Timer or watchdog
- USART activity (in Sleep mode)

Use Cases:

- Sleep mode between sensor readings
- Standby mode during long idle periods
- Stop mode in wearable devices for longer battery life

Do and Don't Section

Do:

- Select the lowest possible mode without affecting functionality
- Use wake-up sources effectively for responsiveness
- Profile power usage across modes for optimal strategy

Don't:

- Rely only on sleep if deeper modes are more effective
- Forget to reinitialize peripherals after deep sleep
- Ignore latency requirements for wake-up

Beginner Tip: Think of low power modes like putting your microcontroller to nap — how deep it sleeps depends on how soon it needs to wake up and what it should remember.

Final Thought: Low power modes are essential for energy-efficient embedded design. Understanding how and when to use each mode can significantly improve battery life and system performance.

Interview Question 93: How Do You Perform Firmware Updates Over-the-Air (OTA)?

Why This Question Is Asked: OTA updates are essential for modern connected devices. This question assesses your knowledge of update mechanisms, wireless communication protocols, and security practices in embedded systems.

What the Interviewer Wants to Know:

- Do you understand the architecture of OTA updates?
- Can you describe the process and technologies involved?
- Are you aware of security, rollback, and error-handling considerations?

How to Structure Your Answer:

1. Define OTA and its importance
2. Explain the general workflow
3. Describe common communication methods and protocols
4. Discuss best practices and precautions

Sample Answer: "Over-the-air (OTA) firmware updates allow embedded devices to receive and install new firmware remotely using wireless communication such as Wi-Fi, Bluetooth, or cellular. The process involves downloading a firmware binary, verifying its integrity, and writing it to flash memory with fallback mechanisms."

Typical OTA Update Workflow:

1. Device connects to server (HTTP/S, MQTT, FTP, etc.)
2. Checks for new firmware version
3. Downloads binary to a temporary memory region
4. Verifies integrity (e.g., checksum, digital signature)
5. Flashes new firmware to active or alternate partition
6. Reboots and runs new firmware
7. Rolls back if update fails

Common Communication Protocols:

- **Wi-Fi:** Most common for IoT devices (ESP32, STM32 + Wi-Fi)
- **Bluetooth (BLE):** Short-range devices like wearables
- **LoRa/Cellular:** Remote devices with limited access
- **MQTT/HTTP(S):** Common OTA update protocols

OTA Bootloader Requirements:

- Dual-partition flash structure (active/backup)
- Update flag or metadata storage in flash/EEPROM
- Safe bootloader that can switch or rollback if needed

Security Best Practices:

- Use encrypted connections (TLS/HTTPS)
- Sign firmware with digital certificates
- Verify authenticity before flashing
- Prevent downgrades and replay attacks

Do and Don't Section

Do:

- Use secure communication protocols
- Include rollback and recovery mechanisms
- Validate firmware before applying it

Don't:

- Flash firmware without integrity checks
- Interrupt update process without a fail-safe
- Leave OTA server unprotected or unauthenticated

Beginner Tip: Think of OTA like remote software updates for your phone — only for embedded devices that may live in hard-to-reach places.

Final Thought: OTA updates improve device longevity and security. A well-implemented OTA strategy ensures seamless maintenance and user satisfaction while minimizing service downtime and manual intervention.

Interview Question 94: What Are Best Practices for Embedded Firmware Development?

Why This Question Is Asked: Embedded firmware must be efficient, reliable, and maintainable. This question assesses your experience and discipline in writing production-quality code for microcontroller-based systems.

What the Interviewer Wants to Know:

- Are you familiar with structured development approaches?
- Do you understand how to reduce bugs and improve maintainability?
- Can you ensure scalability and robustness in firmware design?

How to Structure Your Answer:

1. Cover planning and design practices
2. Explain coding conventions and modularity
3. Describe testing and debugging strategies
4. Mention documentation, version control, and optimization

Sample Answer: "Best practices in embedded firmware development include modular design, use of version control, thorough testing (unit and integration), adherence to coding standards, and efficient resource management. These ensure the firmware is reliable, scalable, and easy to maintain."

1. Design and Architecture:

- Define clear system requirements and use cases
- Use finite state machines (FSMs) for control logic
- Break down functionality into manageable modules
- Plan for memory constraints and timing accuracy

2. Coding Practices:

- Follow coding standards (e.g., MISRA C for safety-critical systems)
- Use meaningful naming conventions and comments
- Avoid magic numbers; use constants or enums
- Prefer modular and reusable code

3. Version Control and Configuration Management:

- Use Git or another VCS to track changes
- Maintain structured repositories (firmware, documentation, scripts)
- Tag stable builds and track release versions

4. Testing and Debugging:

- Write unit tests for drivers and core logic
- Perform integration testing on target hardware

- Use in-circuit debugging, breakpoints, and watch windows
- Employ simulation tools for early-stage logic validation

5. Documentation and Maintenance:

- Document APIs, state machines, memory maps, and dependencies
- Maintain README and changelogs for each release
- Write setup guides for team or field engineers

6. Optimization and Safety:

- Profile memory and CPU usage
- Manage stack/heap usage and avoid fragmentation
- Use watchdog timers and assert statements
- Design for graceful error handling and safe recovery

Do and Don't Section

Do:

- Use static analysis tools and linters
- Separate hardware abstraction from application logic
- Schedule regular code reviews

Don't:

- Mix interrupt logic with business logic
- Hardcode delays without reason
- Ignore power management and fault tolerance

Beginner Tip: Firmware is like writing the soul of a machine — plan it like a blueprint, write it like a story, and test it like a scientist.

Final Thought: Following firmware development best practices improves code quality, reduces bugs, and ensures your embedded systems are scalable and reliable across product life cycles.

Interview Question 95: What Is a Bootloader and How Does It Work?

Why This Question Is Asked: Bootloaders are essential for firmware deployment, system startup, and updates. This question evaluates your understanding of embedded system initialization and secure firmware handling.

What the Interviewer Wants to Know:

- Can you define what a bootloader is?
- Do you understand the steps it performs?
- Are you familiar with use cases like OTA updates, dual firmware, and secure boot?

How to Structure Your Answer:

1. Define a bootloader
2. Describe its role during system startup
3. Explain common features and mechanisms
4. Mention best practices and security concerns

Sample Answer: "A bootloader is a small program that runs immediately after a microcontroller resets or powers up. It is responsible for initializing essential hardware and loading the main firmware application into memory. Bootloaders can also handle firmware upgrades, especially over-the-air (OTA), and enable secure boot mechanisms."

Key Responsibilities of a Bootloader:

- Initialize clocks, memory, and I/O (minimal setup)
- Verify integrity and authenticity of main firmware (optional but recommended)
- Load main application from a known flash location
- Optionally support firmware upgrade interfaces (e.g., UART, USB, OTA)
- Provide fallback or rollback in case of a failed update

Types of Bootloaders:

- **ROM Bootloader:** Pre-installed by chip vendor, unmodifiable
- **User Bootloader:** Custom bootloader programmed into flash
- **Secure Bootloader:** Includes cryptographic verification of firmware

Boot Process Flow:

1. MCU resets or powers on
2. Bootloader runs from a predefined flash region
3. Checks for update mode or triggers (e.g., button press, flag)
4. Validates firmware (optional checksum/signature)
5. Jumps to the application start address

Use Cases:

- Field firmware upgrades via USB/UART/OTA
- Dual bank flash for fail-safe upgrades
- Encrypted firmware and secure authentication

Best Practices:

- Keep bootloader small and simple
- Lock bootloader memory regions to prevent tampering
- Verify firmware with CRC or digital signature before execution
- Use timeout-based fallback to prevent boot lock-up

Do and Don't Section

Do:

- Include version metadata and rollback logic
- Use watchdog timers during update to prevent freeze
- Protect bootloader code with readout protection

Don't:

- Allow unrestricted firmware flashing without verification
- Combine application and bootloader code in the same region
- Depend on unvalidated user inputs to switch modes

Beginner Tip: A bootloader is like a security guard at the system's entrance — it makes sure the code is safe, authentic, and ready to run before handing over control.

Final Thought: A reliable bootloader ensures robust startup and secure firmware management in embedded systems. Understanding its design and function is key to enabling safe updates and stable product deployment.

Interview Question 96: How Do You Handle Faults in Embedded Systems?

Why This Question Is Asked: Fault tolerance is critical for ensuring reliability in embedded systems, especially in safety-critical or industrial applications. This question evaluates your ability to identify, isolate, and respond to errors in a robust way.

What the Interviewer Wants to Know:

- Can you recognize and categorize faults?
- Do you know how to detect, log, and recover from them?
- Are you familiar with software and hardware strategies for fault handling?

How to Structure Your Answer:

1. Define types of faults (hardware, software, external)
2. Explain how to detect and isolate faults
3. Describe techniques for fault response and recovery
4. Mention best practices for logging and debugging

Sample Answer: "Fault handling in embedded systems involves detecting unexpected conditions such as hardware failures, software bugs, or environmental noise, and responding in a way that preserves safety and stability. This includes using watchdog timers, error logs, and reset mechanisms to either recover gracefully or alert the system."

Types of Faults:

- **Hardware Faults:** Power glitches, sensor malfunctions, memory corruption
- **Software Faults:** Stack overflows, NULL pointer dereference, logic errors
- **Communication Faults:** Data corruption, timeouts, protocol mismatches
- **External Faults:** EMI, overheating, voltage fluctuations

Fault Detection Techniques:

- Use of **watchdog timers** for system hangs
- **Assertions** to catch unexpected states during development
- **CRC checks** for memory and communication integrity
- Monitoring **return values**, exceptions, and interrupts
- **Stack overflow guards** and memory protection units (MPU)

Response and Recovery Strategies:

- **Fail-Safe States:** Move to a safe operating condition
- **System Reset:** Soft or hard reset to restore normal operation
- **Redundancy:** Duplicate sensors, communication channels
- **Retry Logic:** Retransmission of commands or reinitialization of peripherals
- **Logging and Alerts:** Store fault codes in EEPROM or send via UART

Example Mechanisms:

- Use of `assert()` macros in debugging builds
- Watchdog-based recovery in production builds
- Fault handler vector in ARM Cortex-M (HardFault_Handler, MemManage_Handler)

Best Practices:

- Separate fault detection from recovery logic
- Test for boundary conditions and rare edge cases
- Document fault conditions and how they are handled

Do and Don't Section

Do:

- Use circular logs or event queues to retain fault history
- Implement diagnostics for post-mortem analysis
- Plan fault trees and mitigation flows in system design

Don't:

- Ignore minor faults that may accumulate into system failure
- Disable watchdogs or fault interrupts without redundancy
- Over-rely on resets without investigating root causes

Beginner Tip: Think of fault handling like a safety net — it won't stop all problems from happening, but it helps you recover before hitting the ground.

Final Thought: Robust fault handling is the cornerstone of reliable embedded systems. By detecting, logging, and recovering from faults effectively, you ensure system stability, user trust, and long-term product success.

Interview Question 97: What Is RTOS? Give Examples

Why This Question Is Asked: Real-Time Operating Systems (RTOS) are commonly used in time-sensitive embedded applications. This question evaluates your understanding of task management, real-time constraints, and multitasking in embedded development.

What the Interviewer Wants to Know:

- Can you define an RTOS and explain how it differs from a general-purpose OS?
- Are you familiar with its key components and benefits?
- Can you give examples and use cases where an RTOS is ideal?

How to Structure Your Answer:

1. Define RTOS and explain its characteristics
2. List core components and scheduling mechanisms
3. Provide real-world examples and applications
4. Mention popular RTOS platforms

Sample Answer: "An RTOS (Real-Time Operating System) is an operating system designed to process data and respond to inputs within a guaranteed time frame. Unlike general-purpose OSes, an RTOS ensures deterministic task scheduling and is used in embedded systems where timing is critical."

Key Characteristics of an RTOS:

- Deterministic task scheduling (hard or soft real-time)
- Multitasking with context switching
- Preemptive or cooperative scheduling
- Priority-based task management
- Real-time synchronization (semaphores, mutexes, queues)

Core Components:

- **Kernel:** Manages tasks, scheduling, and interrupts
- **Task Scheduler:** Allocates CPU time based on priority
- **Inter-task Communication:** Message queues, events, shared memory
- **Timers and Clocks:** Track and schedule real-time operations
- **Memory Management:** Fixed or dynamic allocation with protection

Popular RTOS Examples:

- **FreeRTOS:** Lightweight, open-source, widely used in ARM Cortex-M
- **RT-Thread:** Modular, scalable RTOS for IoT
- **Zephyr OS:** Linux Foundation supported, scalable and secure
- **CMSIS-RTOS:** ARM's standard for real-time APIs (e.g., RTX)
- **ThreadX (Azure RTOS):** Certified for safety-critical applications
- **VxWorks:** Commercial RTOS used in aerospace and automotive

Use Cases:

- Automotive systems (ABS, ECU)
- Industrial control systems
- Medical devices (monitors, pumps)
- Consumer electronics (smart watches, appliances)
- IoT devices with concurrent tasks (communication, sensors, UI)

Do and Don't Section

Do:

- Use RTOS for systems with multiple concurrent real-time tasks
- Leverage queues and semaphores for safe inter-task communication
- Profile system for worst-case timing behavior

Don't:

- Use RTOS when simple superloop architecture suffices
- Mismanage priorities or create resource starvation
- Overuse dynamic memory without proper bounds

Beginner Tip: Think of an RTOS like a traffic cop for tasks — it ensures every task gets through the intersection on time, especially the high-priority ones.

Final Thought: RTOS platforms enable structured multitasking and timing accuracy in complex embedded systems. Knowing when and how to use them helps you build responsive, reliable applications for real-time environments.

Interview Question 98: How Is Task Scheduling Handled in RTOS?

Why This Question Is Asked: Task scheduling is the backbone of any real-time operating system. This question tests your understanding of how RTOS manages task execution to meet timing and priority constraints.

What the Interviewer Wants to Know:

- Do you understand scheduling types and policies?
- Can you explain how tasks get prioritized and switched?
- Are you familiar with preemptive vs cooperative multitasking?

How to Structure Your Answer:
1. Explain what task scheduling means in RTOS
2. Describe different scheduling algorithms
3. Discuss task states and context switching
4. Provide RTOS examples (e.g., FreeRTOS, Zephyr)

Sample Answer: "Task scheduling in an RTOS determines which task should run at any moment based on priority, state, and timing requirements. It ensures that critical tasks meet their deadlines while efficiently using the CPU."

Key Concepts in RTOS Task Scheduling:

- **Task Prioritization:** Each task has a priority; higher-priority tasks run first
- **Preemptive Scheduling:** A running task can be interrupted by a higher-priority task
- **Cooperative Scheduling:** Tasks voluntarily yield control to the scheduler
- **Time Slicing (Round Robin):** Equal priority tasks share CPU time in slices

Task States:

1. **Running:** Task currently executing
2. **Ready:** Eligible to run, waiting for CPU
3. **Blocked:** Waiting for an event (e.g., semaphore, delay)
4. **Suspended:** Not eligible to run

Scheduling Algorithms:

- **Fixed Priority Preemptive Scheduling:** (e.g., FreeRTOS default)
- **Earliest Deadline First (EDF):** Tasks scheduled based on deadlines
- **Rate Monotonic Scheduling (RMS):** Shorter periods = higher priority
- **Round Robin:** Equal CPU time for same-priority tasks

Context Switching:

- Happens when the scheduler stops one task and starts another
- Involves saving and restoring CPU registers, stack pointers, and PC
- Managed by RTOS kernel, often triggered by interrupts or system calls

Example (FreeRTOS):

- xTaskCreate() creates tasks with specific priorities
- vTaskDelay() or blocking on xQueueReceive() moves task to Blocked state
- Scheduler decides next Ready task to run

Do:

- Assign task priorities based on real-time requirements
- Avoid priority inversion by using mutexes with priority inheritance
- Use blocking APIs (e.g., queues, semaphores) instead of polling

Don't:

- Let low-priority tasks starve high-frequency tasks
- Block high-priority tasks for long durations
- Use tight loops or delays in tasks without yielding CPU

Beginner Tip: Think of RTOS scheduling like organizing a concert — the performers (tasks) must follow a strict time and priority plan so the show runs smoothly.

Final Thought: Efficient task scheduling is key to predictable and responsive RTOS-based systems. A good grasp of scheduling policies and task behavior leads to high-performance and reliable embedded applications.

Interview Question 99: What Is Priority Inversion?

Why This Question Is Asked: Priority inversion is a classic concurrency problem in real-time systems. This question tests your understanding of task scheduling issues and your ability to apply synchronization solutions in embedded environments.

What the Interviewer Wants to Know:

- Can you explain what priority inversion is and why it's a problem?
- Do you understand when and how it occurs?
- Are you familiar with methods to prevent or resolve it?

How to Structure Your Answer:

1. Define priority inversion and describe the conditions for it
2. Explain its impact in real-time systems
3. Describe resolution techniques such as priority inheritance
4. Use examples to clarify the concept

Sample Answer: "Priority inversion occurs when a low-priority task holds a shared resource needed by a high-priority task, and a medium-priority task preempts the low-priority one, blocking the high-priority task indirectly. This can cause critical timing issues in real-time systems."

How Priority Inversion Happens:

1. **Low-priority Task** holds a mutex
2. **High-priority Task** gets blocked waiting for the mutex
3. **Medium-priority Task** runs, preventing the low-priority task from releasing the mutex
4. High-priority task is stuck waiting on a lower-priority one

Why It's Dangerous:

- Breaks the expected priority-based execution order
- Can cause missed deadlines in real-time systems
- Difficult to debug because the high-priority task appears idle

Example Scenario:
- Low-priority task writes to a shared log file (mutex locked)
- High-priority task needs to log a fault (blocks)
- Medium-priority task handles communication (runs repeatedly)
- High-priority task waits indefinitely

Solutions:
- **Priority Inheritance Protocol:** Temporarily raises the priority of the low-priority task to that of the blocked high-priority task
- **Priority Ceiling Protocol:** Mutexes have a predefined ceiling priority; tasks must have equal or higher priority to lock them
- **Avoid shared resource blocking in high-priority tasks**

RTOS Support:

- FreeRTOS supports priority inheritance with mutexes (xSemaphoreCreateMutex())
- Other RTOSes like VxWorks and ThreadX also implement similar mechanisms

Do and Don't Section

Do:

- Use mutexes that support priority inheritance for shared resources
- Design critical sections to be as short as possible
- Profile task priorities and shared resource access paths

Don't:

- Ignore possible interactions between tasks of different priorities
- Hold locks in low-priority tasks for long durations
- Disable priority inheritance in systems where timing is critical

Beginner Tip: Priority inversion is like a slow car blocking an ambulance — unless you clear the road, the emergency can't proceed.

Final Thought: Understanding and preventing priority inversion is vital for building reliable real-time embedded systems. Proper task design and synchronization primitives ensure predictable behavior even under high concurrency.

Interview Question 100: How Do You Secure an Embedded System?

Why This Question Is Asked: Security is increasingly important in embedded systems, especially with the rise of IoT. This question evaluates your understanding of embedded system vulnerabilities and the strategies you use to protect devices from cyber threats and tampering.

What the Interviewer Wants to Know:

- Are you aware of common embedded system threats?
- Can you describe layered security approaches?
- Do you understand secure boot, encryption, and firmware protection?

How to Structure Your Answer:

1. Identify key security challenges
2. Describe hardware and software security measures
3. Explain secure firmware and communication practices
4. Mention real-world examples or protocols

Sample Answer: "Securing an embedded system involves protecting data, firmware, and communication channels through encryption, authentication, access control, and secure boot mechanisms. A layered approach using both hardware and software techniques is essential to defend against attacks."

Common Threats to Embedded Systems:

- Unauthorized firmware access or modification
- Data interception or tampering (e.g., man-in-the-middle attacks)
- Debug interface misuse (e.g., JTAG, UART)
- Firmware reverse engineering or code extraction
- Physical tampering and side-channel attacks

Security Techniques:

1. Secure Boot:

- Verifies digital signature of firmware before execution
- Ensures only authenticated code is executed

2. Encryption:

- Encrypt firmware images and communication channels (e.g., AES,

TLS)
- Store sensitive data in encrypted flash or EEPROM

3. Access Control:

- Disable or password-protect debug interfaces (JTAG, SWD)
- Restrict bootloader access to authorized channels only

4. Firmware Protection:

- Read-out protection (ROP) or memory access lock
- Code obfuscation to prevent reverse engineering
- Use of secure microcontrollers with TrustZone or secure elements

5. Communication Security:

- Use secure protocols (TLS, SSH, MQTT-S)
- Implement mutual authentication between device and server

6. Regular Updates and OTA Security:

- Digitally sign updates and verify before flashing
- Use rollback protection and fail-safe recovery
- Validate version numbers and update sources

Best Practices:

- Perform threat modeling during system design
- Minimize attack surface (remove unused ports/features)
- Log and monitor system behavior for intrusion detection

Do and Don't Section

Do:

- Use hardware security features built into MCUs (e.g., STM32H7 RDP, Secure Boot)
- Regularly audit and update firmware

- Encrypt sensitive configuration data at rest and in transit

Don't:

- Leave debug interfaces exposed in production devices
- Store passwords or keys in plain text
- Ignore physical security if the device is deployed in the field

Beginner Tip: Think of embedded system security like securing a smart home — lock the doors (firmware), encrypt the Wi-Fi (communication), and monitor for break-ins (anomaly detection).

Final Thought: Securing embedded systems requires a proactive, defense-in-depth strategy. Understanding both hardware and software protections is essential for ensuring the long-term integrity and trustworthiness of your embedded devices.

Interview Question 101: Describe a Small Project You've Built Using an Embedded System

Why This Question Is Asked: This question helps interviewers assess your hands-on experience, problem-solving skills, and familiarity with embedded development tools and workflows.

What the Interviewer Wants to Know:

- Can you clearly describe an embedded project you've worked on?
- Do you understand hardware-software integration?
- Did you face any challenges and how did you solve them?

How to Structure Your Answer:

1. Introduce the project idea and goals
2. List the hardware and software components used
3. Describe implementation steps and key features
4. Discuss challenges and what you learned

Sample Answer: "I built a smart plant monitoring system using an ESP32 microcontroller. The goal was to monitor soil moisture and temperature, and send alerts to a mobile app when the plant needed watering. It was a low-cost, battery-powered IoT device designed for home automation."

Project Overview:

- **Microcontroller:** ESP32 (Wi-Fi & BLE enabled)
- **Sensors:** DHT11 for temperature/humidity, capacitive soil moisture sensor
- **Power Source:** 3.7V Li-Ion battery with TP4056 charging module
- **Display:** OLED screen (I2C)
- **Communication:** Blynk app over Wi-Fi for real-time notifications

Key Features:

- Periodic data logging to cloud
- OLED display shows real-time readings
- Battery voltage monitoring and power-saving sleep mode
- Mobile alerts when moisture drops below threshold

Development Tools:

- Arduino IDE with ESP32 board support
- Blynk mobile app for IoT dashboard
- GitHub for version control

Challenges Faced:

- Calibrating the moisture sensor for different soil types
- Power optimization to ensure long battery life
- Handling Wi-Fi disconnections gracefully

What I Learned:

- Importance of low-power design techniques (deep sleep mode)
- Benefits of modular coding for readability and reuse
- Real-world limitations of inexpensive sensors and how to compensate with software filtering

Do and Don't Section

Do:

- Focus on what you contributed technically
- Highlight problem-solving and iterative testing
- Share what you learned and what you'd improve next time

Don't:

- Overcomplicate your explanation
- Downplay bugs or challenges — show how you solved them
- Forget to mention testing and validation steps

Beginner Tip: Even a simple project can demonstrate strong embedded skills if you show clear goals, solid design choices, and practical troubleshooting.

Final Thought: Describing a project well proves not just your technical knowledge, but your ability to think critically, adapt, and deliver results in embedded systems development.

www.ingramcontent.com/pod-product-compliance
Lightning Source LLC
LaVergne TN
LVHW051325050326
832903LV00031B/3371